Student to CEO

97 ways to influence your way to the top ir

STUDENT TO CEO

97 Ways To Influence Your Way To The Top In
Banking & Finance

SIMON DIXON

Student to CEO

First published in 2011 by

Ecademy Press

48 St Vincent Drive, St Albans, Herts, AL1 5SJ

info@ecademy-press.com

www.ecademy-press.com

Printed and Bound by Lightning Source in the UK and USA

Set in Palatino and Myriad by Karen Gladwell

Cover artwork Jal Islam

Printed on acid-free paper from managed forests. This book is printed on demand, so no copies will be remaindered or pulped.

ISBN 978-1-907722-18-9

Contents

What Others Are Saying About This Book...

"Having built a successful career in trading, I wish that I had been handed this book when I was a student, my path to success would have been cut in half. Simon shows you step by step how to make it in banking and finance the entrepreneurial way and build a brand, rather than a job. This will save you years."

Tom Hougaard, world famous trader and founder of www.whichwaytoday.com as seen on Bloomberg, CNN and BBC.

"Having spent a year with the biggest Chicago pit traders and seen first hand how careers have been destroyed or super-charged due to changes in how to climb to the top in trading, those who have survived the changes have adapted using some of the strategies that Simon Dixon outlines in this book.

I would love to give a copy of this book to all the traders that I know who have experienced less fortune. A great guide to both the psychology and strategy of the most successful in banking and finance and a must read for any ambitious student."

James Allen Smith, Director of the movie 'Floored' based on the true stories of Chicago floor traders.

"An invaluable guide to making it big in banking and finance. Written specifically for the new generation graduate trying to make sense of the post credit crunch economy, it takes a truly original approach to careers advice. Rather than churning out the same old platitudes it gives a step by step guide to success based on genuine insider insights."

Mike Harris, founding CEO of three multi billion pound business including the first internet bank, Egg, and the first telephone bank, First Direct.

What Others Are Saying About This Book...

"After starring in the Million Dollar Traders documentary I am often contacted by students who want to work with me in my Hedge Fund. If only they followed some of the strategies that Simon Dixon outlines in this book, they would stand a much better chance."

Lex van Dam, Hedge Fund Manager and author of 'How To Make Money Trading'.

"A step by step guide for students to accelerate their way to the inner circle in banking and finance. Simon shares how he has gone from student to Key Person of Influence in Banking and Finance and how you can do the same starting now."

Daniel Priestley, author of Become A Key Person Of Influence.

Acknowledgements

This book could not have been written without the loving support of my soul mate and lifelong partner, my wife Bliss Dixon. I would like to thank her for booking the beautiful cottages in Italy to make sure I put the necessary time in to complete this book, as well as putting up with my obsessive behavior in business.

Jal Islam has been a continued source of support for me and as a shareholder in Metal Monkey Private Equity has dedicated considerable time to consulting thousands of students and graduates at Benedix, providing invaluable research on the difference between success and failure from students and graduates.

Thanks to my parents Reg Dixon and Sharon Kaye, who have played an instrumental part of my life journey that has allowed me to arrive at the experiences that have led me to the moment I write this book.

A further thanks go to many of my friends that have achieved great things in banking and finance and have contributed to many of the case studies in this book, especially Mike Harris, the founder of Egg and First Direct, Peter Hargreaves, the founder of Hargreaves Lansdown, James Allen Smith, the creator of the movie *Floored*, Lex van Dam, the founder of the Million Dollar Traders documentary, Daniel Priestley, author of Becoming A Key Person of Influence and Tom Hougaard, the founder of Which Way Today.

This book would never have happened without the support, mentoring and training of the book midwife, Mindy Gibbins Klein.

There are many others that have contributed to the life experience that has led to the passion that I have poured into this book, and I would like to thank you all.

My final thanks go to the many thousands of graduates of my Banking and Finance Professional Program who have provided great feedback and motivation, allowing me to share these ideas with you.

About the Author

Simon Dixon has helped many thousands climb to the top in Banking and Finance after founding the worlds leading training and consultancy company for students and graduates seeking careers in banking and finance, Benedix.

As the founder of Metal Monkey Private Equity and Metal Monkey Enterprise, Simon has become recognised for his contribution towards the development of Banking and Finance.

Through his work with students, he has guest spoke at hundreds of universities and colleges worldwide, as well as being featured on Channel 4, BBC and Bloomberg sharing his journey from tea boy to Stock Broker, to City Trader, to Investment Banker to CEO, all before the age of 30.

As an active campaigner and consultant on the need for banking and monetary reform, he has written for publication like the Financial Times and City AM.

As a CEO of Metal Monkey Enterprise, specialising in new and innovative forms of banking, Simon also works with businesses to help them adapt to market changes.

Introduction

"What kind of a name is Metal Monkey?"

When I see the look on people's faces as I tell them the name of my new banking company, it always brings a smile to my face.

You see, everyone has a path they can take in life. You have a choice now to be a cog in the wheel like most of the world, or you can choose to be the wheel itself.

If you have ambitions of being the wheel, but are struggling as our economy is not producing the right environment to facilitate your goals, there is an alternative. You can create something that makes the wheel obsolete or simply reinvent the wheel yourself.

We all have a choice, yet quite often we forget and kid ourselves into thinking that we have no choice because there is something we cannot control getting in our way.

The obstacles I hear most often from students are: recession; did not go to a top ten university; did not achieve the best grades; lack of experience; not born in the right country; the wrong accent; underprivileged background – or whatever they can hold on to that is out of their control. It is natural to feel this way as we are surrounded by people who have doomed themselves to be a cog in the wheel.

They all have a reason why they are where they are. Most often they believe it is not their fault. These students secretly resent the 'wheels' as they feel they got there through 'luck'. They normally have a good reason why they cannot reinvent the wheel and why that is a game for only the 'lucky' and the 'privileged'.

The problem is that this is a lie. I personally believe that everybody can become the 'wheel' or reinvent the wheel if they choose.

To become a wheel, you cannot do what other cogs do and you certainly cannot follow the advice of other cogs.

By the end of this book my goal is to find out what wheel you are going to become, or what wheel you are going to reinvent. I am writing this book because your achievement in banking is so important to me as you are a huge part of my greater mission in life.

Today is my thirtieth birthday and my wife just handed me the share certificate of my latest venture in banking, 'Metal Monkey'. No ordinary bank, but a bank for the people. The bank is one part of my greater mission.

The first part of my mission is to create a bank for the people. The second part of my mission is the one that gets most people upset or excited – to create a bank for the people under a system that works. In other words, my mission involves reforming our banking and our monetary system.

When you discover your mission, you will be amazed how everything in your life comes together. The fact that you have picked up this book and are reading it right now shows to me that you want something bigger in your life than most.

Now, most people who do not know me look at me a bit funnily when I explain the scale of my mission, and even people who do know me look at me as if to say, "Simon, you're pushing it a bit far this time round!"

When people tell me all the reasons why it is not possible, I know at that moment I am truly living my dreams.

When I explain my mission, I have exact clarity of what I was brought on this earth to do. I know what the next thirty years looks like. I am excited about the future. Most importantly, I know I am spending every day truly living my dreams.

I write these words passionately and excitedly on my thirtieth birthday as this week has truly been a special week, one for which I am really grateful. I look forward to the day when I hear your story of how you arrived at your mission. It was not until this moment of quiet reflection that I realised my mission was becoming a reality.

In the last week I had the opportunity to give an introduction pitch to Mike Harris, the founder of the first telephone bank in the UK, First Direct, and the first internet bank in the world, Egg, about my new banking venture.

After leaving the meeting with Mike Harris at one of the UK's largest VCs, I left with a sense that anything is possible but, just as importantly, a list of contacts to make the mission a reality.

That very same day I got a call from an American documentary producer asking to film me in Bristol on the future of banking and monetary reform, a mission I have been working on for years now.

I then got a call to give an interview and present in Birmingham with Sky TV on the future of banking in response to one of Mervyn King's (the Governor of the Bank of England) speeches, as he starts to hint at banking reform in the way that I have been presenting to the world for the last four years.

Before setting off to enjoy a birthday trip away with my wife, I made a pit-stop to the Mermaid Auditorium in London city where I was invited to present to 500 entrepreneurs and make the first public announcement of my new bank.

As I sit here today on my thirtieth birthday in a beautiful cottage in the countryside of North Wales that the love of my life... my partner for life...my wife Bliss Dixon (this is the same person by the way) booked for us, I thought 'what better time to write the introduction to my new book'.

You see, rewind the clock to ten years ago and my mission was to be an investment banker. After graduating, I went on to suffer over 200 rejections from many banks and financial institutions as I applied during the dot-com bust recession. But through a relentless search for meaning and mission, I discovered that I was here to do something much bigger. I realise now that for thirty years every moment in my life has led to my mission to create an innovative bank for the people under a banking system that works.

This week has now become a typical week for me and my stupid dreams and fantasies are actually happening.

I also think to myself what a difference a decade can make for those who dare to live by their mission.

As I write this book, our banking system is broken, people are suffering depression as our economy is depressing, the government and economists are in denial as we try to fix and patch up a banking system that will never work and I am receiving an average of 50 Facebook messages a day from students who find themselves in an economy that no longer wants them.

I tell the students that all the recession means is huge opportunity for those who adjust to change and that the greatest businesses, breakthroughs and opportunities are born out of a recessive and depressive economy.

Students normally spend several hours going through my books, videos and training programs before they realise how truly exciting today is, and how today is the only time in history that you can go from student to CEO faster than ever by living your mission.

I then show them stories of countless graduates from my programs who have achieved amazing things by adjusting their approach in line with the current environment, who decided to live their life by mission.

Today is the first time I have been on Facebook during my birthday and I had a tear in my eye as I read the wall posts from those whose lives have changed by adopting some of the principles that I outline for you in this book, as they send me 'happy birthday' wishes.

If you want to be a CEO, it's not hard. The quickest way is to register your own company and hire yourself as CEO, as I have with my new bank; how easy is that?

But that is not what this book is about.

This book is designed to share with you the best of my thinking today, and that of many banking leaders in history, on how you can climb the ladder fast, starting with securing your first career in banking and finance.

Throughout this book I will give you countless stories, examples and tools of influence in order for you to discover your mission, purpose and journey from student to CEO.

I know these tools work because I have suffered multiple rejections for jobs in banking and finance and learnt a thing or two in turning it around.

I have also been able to teach these principles to thousands of students and graduates from every background imaginable and test that they work, as these people now work in their ideal roles in banks and financial institutions or own their own investment societies, or started their own businesses in banking and finance.

After almost giving up, I finally started my banking career as a tea boy. Through using these principles I went on to secure careers in stockbroking, trading, investment banking and eventually starting three businesses in banking and finance – from a student consultancy to a trading consultancy to a private equity firm and now, my latest venture, a bank with a twist.

Through my student consultancy, I have presented to and spoken with literally hundreds of thousands of students and there is not a type of person or background that I have not come across. I have seen first-hand that anybody can do it when they integrate certain tools and lessons into their lives.

From working with some of the best traders who trade millions every day through my trading consultancy, I have seen first-hand that success leaves clues.

From meeting world political leaders through my mission to reform money, I have seen that those who make it to the top do things differently from everybody else.

And from having the privilege to partner and work with some of the greatest minds in business through Metal Monkey Private Equity, I have seen first-hand that regardless of background or education, people can achieve remarkable things.

But the encouraging thing is that I came to university in London, UK, knowing nobody and decided that I was going to build my own path.

When you continue to read this book, I will share with you how you can do the same. When you read until the end, you will understand that our lives are exactly what we dare to make them and at the very end you will have a sense of clarity and mission that will excite you with possibilities in a world where most doom themselves to an ordinary life. I don't want you to do the same as everyone else. I don't want you to be a cog in the wheel. I want you to become the wheel, reinvent the wheel or make the wheel obsolete.

So the journey beings now with your map...

CHAPTER ONE

Your Map

He stood there nervously, ironing his shirt; he was remembering how it felt when the letter came through the door with the KBC Peel Hunt Investment Bank logo printed on the front.

To just get the interview he attended two days ago took him over 200 applications, over 100 letters, countless phone calls and meeting after meeting. He felt like there was nothing more of him to give and the thought of yet another rejection was unbearable.

He felt like he had worked so hard at university and he could not understand why he was not getting any offers.

He was so fed up of the rejection letters, he was actually preparing himself mentally for yet another rejection before the letter had even been opened. He found himself pretending that he didn't care anymore and that he didn't want to work for an investment bank anyway.

So he went quietly into his room and tore open the letter. Carelessly he tore the corner of the letter when he tore the envelope open, thinking to himself 'it doesn't matter anyway, it will join the pile of paper on the corner of the desk with all the other rejection letters'.

He anticipated the words 'Unfortunately your application has been unsuccessful this time around, please apply again in the future', but the words read a little strange this time.

He was looking for the 'Unfortunately', but it was not there.

So he read again:

'We are delighted to...'

He stood there, confused, and thought to himself 'surely not...'

As he read, he realised he had just been offered an analyst role at KBC Peel Hunt as a market maker; he was overcome with joy.

As he ran down the stairs to share the good news with his family, he also felt a little nervous.

He read the letter again, just to check they had sent it to the right person and he checked that it was in fact his name on the letter. He read the letter to his father, as his father watched his son proudly share the news. The whole family was overwhelmed with delight as all the hard work had paid off and he had secured himself a top-paying trading role in an investment bank.

"Ouch", he shouted as he came back to the present and the steam coming from the iron burnt his hand.

Today was his first day on the trading floor and he was in nervous anticipation.

The iron was approaching the end of its life and water began to leak out all over the new TM Lewin shirt he had bought for his first day on the trading floor.

He did not know what to expect and finished ironing, trying to dry the wet patch on his shirt as he finished dressing himself in a new Paul Smith suit he had bought with his staff discount from Selfridges, and a matching tie. As he tied the laces on his brand new Ted Baker black shiny shoes, he noticed they were a little stiff and made him walk a bit strangely.

The soles were slippery as they had not seen the pavement before and he tried to balance himself after a little skid as he shut the gate behind him.

As the gate slammed closed he pulled out his new employment contract for one last check before he hit the tube.

He hopped on to the Northern line and counted the stops to Moorgate station.

As the train approached Moorgate, he found himself crushed in the corner as suit after suit jumped on the tube and filled every available space.

Finally they arrived at Moorgate station and he lurched out of the tube doors as they opened abruptly. Like an ant trail, he climbed the stairs, forced forward with the crowd.

As he made his way to the top of the stairs everything was unfamiliar.

He did not realise there were multiple exits at Moorgate station as, confused, he read the signs posted with unfamiliar landmarks. King William Street? Lombard Street? Bank of England? Bakerloo line?

As he headed for the nearest exit he found himself surrounded by business men and business women, all of whom seemed to know where they were going.

It dawned upon him that he had no idea where he was.

So he pulled out his paperwork from his inside jacket pocket while he looked for a quiet corner out of everybody's way.

He shuffled through the paperwork and could not find the printed directions he had prepared the night before, detailing how to get to the office.

Unfortunately this was before the iPhone and Google Maps were invented.

All of a sudden, he realised he had forgotten to bring his paperwork with the office address on it.

A feeling of panic overwhelmed him as he pictured the terrifying thought of being late on his first day.

Collecting his thoughts, he decided that help was needed and asked a passer-by where the nearest tube to 111 Old Broad Street was.

To his horror, he found out that he was not meant to get off at Moorgate station and that Bank was the nearest station.

Quickly, he held out his hand and signalled over a black cab as he tried to stuff his paperwork back into his jacket pocket.

"To 111 Old Broad Street," he shouted.

After speaking with the cab driver, it turned out that Moorgate station and Bank station were within five minutes' walk of each other. Not wanting to take any risks, he waited in a traffic jam for 20 minutes and paid the cabby £17 to take him right to the front door.

He arrived in good time and headed to the bathroom to calm his nerves before reporting to reception.

He had arrived early for his first day as a market maker.

How do I know such graphic detail, you ask? Because it happened to someone I know better than anybody else – me.

As I reflect upon my first day at my new job when I could not find my way from Moorgate station to Bank station, paralysed with fear of being late, I thought to myself what a difference a few years can make when you are focused.

Forward on a few years and I am truly living my dreams.

When I worked in retail at Selfridges, I had dreams of being a high flier in the City.

I had dreams, but I didn't really know what I wanted or how to get it. I thought that everyone who worked in the City was a big-time trader and imagined myself there one day, but never really knew how.

The thought of being CEO of my own private equity company or starting a bank, as I did a few years later, was nothing but a pipe dream.

I got my first break in banking and finance as a tea boy at stockbrokers TD Waterhouse. I never really made it the traditional way as I did not tick all the boxes.

But before I get into how my dreams became a reality and how you can do the same whatever your background, perhaps there might be a bit more to my 'first day of work at an investment bank' story than meets the eye.

In fact there is.

Although you may never make the same mistake as I did on my first day at my new banking and finance job, I am almost certain that you have made the same mistake as me at some point in your life.

There is a hidden mistake that 99% of students and graduates, including myself, make which prevents them from ever getting their first offer in banking and finance, let alone climb to the top. In fact, it gets them rejected time and time again; it also retracts all opportunity from them as they meet useful contacts.

Let's dig a little bit deeper.

In order to guarantee that you get to where you want to go, you need three components.

If you do not know the way then you need a map, right?

Well, nowadays this could be a Google app on an iPhone, or whatever Steve Jobs and the new age entrepreneurs come out with next to make life easier for us.

But will any map do?

Of course not, it must be the right map for the area in which we are travelling. I have found that most people in planning their path to the top in banking and finance are following the wrong map.

When I suffered from multiple rejections, I learnt this the hard way. I was asking everybody around me to help me to secure my first career in banking and finance, none of whom had secured a career in banking and finance, let alone achieved to a high level.

Yes, they were qualified careers advisors and seemed to know all the deadlines and application processes, but it had not worked out for me, despite following all the application tips and CV workshops and company presentation advice.

When I realised I was asking those who had not achieved the result I wanted, I immediately sought the advice of banking and finance professionals on how to get my foot in the door.

Everyone seemed willing to give me an opinion and share their take. While the banking and finance professionals' map was different from everybody else's, I noticed something strange.

Those who loved, and I mean loved their job, and had made it to the top, seemed to have a completely different map from those who had just secured a job in banking and finance.

So I soon realised that the map you follow is very important. Just as a map of Chicago would be useless in London, I have found that the maps of those who have not climbed to the top in banking and finance are as useless as a map of Chicago in London.

But let's say that we have found the right map or we now carry around our iPhone with Google Maps on it.

Think about it, the map has no use at all if we don't know where we are.

I experienced this when I got off at Moorgate station all those years ago. Now in hindsight, I could have run back into the tube station and looked at the local map that you normally find on the wall of all tube stations, but because I had no idea where I was I didn't even know that I was just around the corner from Bank station and that there was a perfectly good map available in the station.

So because Google Maps did not have a mobile app back then I took the safe option and got in a cab.

I have found that most students and graduates do not know how far away they are after finishing university in terms of having what is required to climb to the top in banking and finance because they have been in the books getting advice from professors for too long.

As you have probably experienced already, I found this out the hard way too, when I was told how far off I was after completing my Masters.

Luckily, on my first day of work I remembered the office address. For some reason, 111 Old Broad Street stuck in my mind and the cab driver knew where it was, as well as knowing where we were.

But because I did not know it was five minutes' walk, it cost me 20 minutes and £17 to get there.

Experience tells me that students and graduates take the long way round and the more expensive route – that is if they ever get there at all, because they do not know where they are going.

During my university road show where I was presenting to up to 5,000 students and graduates a month, on earning more, achieving more and getting more offers in banking and finance, I would say the number one reason they do not climb to the top in banking and finance is because they do not know what they want, are unfocused and cannot communicate exactly where they are going, what they are studying for and what career lights them up.

While I was getting multiple rejections, I was applying for every job that had the words 'banking and finance' in it, from trading to auditing, from corporate finance to cashier, from accountant to fund management and everything in between.

If you want to climb to the top in banking and finance and go from student to CEO fast, you will need to lay a strong foundation.

You need a map that has come from someone who has gone from student to CEO fast, and who is willing to share it with you.

You need to know where you are right now, so you can start making the necessary changes, and you need to know specifically and precisely what career in banking and finance you want, to lay your plan for climbing to the top.

If you choose to accept, I would like to show you how I did it and how you can do the same.

In this book you will get three things: a map that works, modelled from the top 1% of achievers in banking and finance; an understanding of where you are right now and what you need to do to begin your journey; and you will gain clarity on where you want to go so you can climb to the top.

Interwoven between those three main outcomes you will be given the tools to make sure you do it, follow through on your goals, as well as the tools of influence you will need to make it a reality – in fact 97 of them.

Throughout the book, I include inspirational stories from those who have already left their legacy in banking and finance, with my take on how they did it and, most importantly, how you can do it too.

So here are influence tools one to three.

Influence Tool 1
Know your outcome

Influence Tool 2
*Know where you are right
now in relation to your goals*

Influence Tool 3
Model success from the top

Having dedicated the last ten years of my life (at the time of writing) to the study and application of success and failure in banking and finance, having gone from student to CEO before the age of thirty, having worked with tens of thousands of students and graduates across the world, having the privilege of working alongside the top 1% in the industry, I have come to realise that there are similarities in those who go to the top and those who don't even get their first offer.

I have also come to realise that if you are focused enough and determined enough, your grades, degree, visa status, experience level, university and the countless other things that students and graduates tend to see as barriers do not matter.

These barriers are speed bumps that slow you down in your journey but, one by one, you slow down and drive over them until you hit the motorway where all speed bumps disappear and new problems arise, such as fast-breaking cars and road rage.

When you meet those top 1% in banking and finance, you realise that they overcame a lot of the same problems that you see as barriers today.

The key is: are you willing to accept full responsibility for your achievement and let go of any excuses that you might have been using in order to protect yourself from any more rejection?

Influence Tool 4
Accept full responsibility for your achievement

I have noticed that the top 1% accept responsibility for everything, even when it is not their fault, because that way they can control it, rather than feeling helpless. They are masters of driving over speed bumps and facing obstacles head on.

They find a way time and time again, even though they are faced with problems all the way.

The problems are always there, it is the meaning that you give to these problems and how you overcome them that will allow you to climb to the top in banking and finance fast.

Throughout this book I give examples of those who have shaped the modern world of banking and finance as we know it today so you can be armed with lots of maps from past achievers.

I provide these maps as a model of success for you. The concept of modelling success is one that has allowed me to compress decades of experience into weeks.

It is the primary principle that has allowed me to live my dreams before my thirtieth birthday.

It is the simple concept of finding those top 1% of achievers, putting yourself in a position of value whereby they are willing to help you, and modelling how they think psychologically and strategically with your own twist added.

You will find that they do things differently from the 99% of people who never live their definition of success. When you enter this world, you will see that success leaves clues.

Use these 97 ways to influence your way to the top and your journey from student to CEO will be fast.

They provide a map modelled from the success of the top 1% of achievers, and they can be used by you too.

The tools outlined in this book have been used by countless students and graduates to climb the ladder fast in banking and finance, and there is no reason why they cannot do the same for you.

This book has been written to give you a map of how to go from to student to CEO, no matter what your background may be.

So let's begin this journey with a quick exercise before we move on to Influence Tool 5.

Exercise 1

Answer these questions without doing any further research, just jot down your first answer.

If you do not know the answer, then that is the answer.

Later you can replace the answers with better ones or confirm that you have, in fact, written the correct answer for you.

The answers are your own and nobody else's.

1. **Where in banking and finance do I want to work?**

2. **What do I have right now that makes me the ideal candidate for this role?**

3. **Who do I know who has achieved to the top in that role?**

4. **Who could I know who has achieved to the top in this role?**

5. **What would I have to do to attract this person to be my mentor?**

If you were struggling to answer any of these questions, register for a free Webinar by visiting :

www.benedix.co.uk/simon-dixon-webinar

Now that you have an initial guide for where you are, where you want to be and how you might get a map to achieve your goal, you are ready for Influence Tool 5. Ignoring this tool is responsible for more failed applications, more rejections and more frustration than any other.

Use this tool to its full potential and your journey to the top in banking and finance will have already begun...

CHAPTER TWO

Know What You Want

influence your way to the top in banking and finance

Influence Tool 5
Focus your efforts

"I want to work in banking and finance."

For a second right now, imagine you are the Managing Director of the investment banking division at a boutique investment bank.

You have been assigned the job of finding that student or graduate who is going to make a difference in your division, the graduate who can immediately get started putting together pitch books and completing due diligence reports, who can quickly bring in new business and start quickly bringing in more revenue than you have to pay them in wages.

Influence Tool 6
Be worth more than you get paid

You have thousands of CVs to go through, you don't know where to begin.

You get a whole load of CVs from people who simply list everything they have done in the past and discuss their desire to work for a company like yours (if they get that far) and what they studied at university.

Then, for some reason, a CV catches your eye. As you dig deeper, you notice their track record of bringing in new business for their university finance society, their portfolio of stocks that they have invested in because they have calculated them to be undervalued, their professional qualification in investment banking, their desire to work for a boutique investment bank in the corporate finance division because of their networks and you notice the information is presented in the form of a pitch book rather than a CV.

Influence Tool 7
Results are more powerful than words on your CV (and I'm not talking academic grades)

Would you at least be curious and call them for an interview above everyone else who is pitching their academic achievements and their list of irrelevant things of which they are proud?

Exactly.

The challenge is, with no experience how can a student or graduate do this?

The answer is focus.

If you know exactly what you are going for, then how hard is it to find a top achiever in that specific field who you can model and develop the skills, results and experience to prove that you are that ideal candidate?

There are three commitments that stop 99% of students and graduates from achieving this result. To climb to the top you will need to:

1. **Commit to mastering your time.**
2. **Commit to finding and following your passion.**
3. **Take control of your beliefs.**

I will discuss all three commitments in this book, but the time commitment is discussed in this chapter. The passion and beliefs sections are the topics of Chapters 3 and 4 respectively.

Your greatest asset, far more than money, is time. The good news is we all have the same amount of time in a day, so nobody is at an advantage here.

How you allocate that time will, however, put you at an advantage.

Influence Tool 8
Invest your time better than anybody else

To get your foot in the door in banking and finance you will need to be in the top 1% of students and graduates.

Before you freak out and give up now, your definition of top 1% may be slightly different from mine.

While most students and university professors define top 1% in terms of academic achievement, grades and university stature, I define top 1% as those who know what they want and are willing to do whatever it takes to achieve it.

My definition applies to any academic background and, in order to qualify, you just need to make a decision to do whatever it takes.

Of those of you who get through to the top 1% and get the job, only another 1% will climb to the top and achieve their definition of success.

A side note here: climbing to the top may not be your definition of success. I am just making this assumption because you picked up and started reading a book called Student to CEO that you have decided that climbing to the top is part of your definition of success.

Influence Tool 9
Live your definition of success, not someone else's

I have also found that very few know what it takes to climb to the top. The good news is that you are doing what 99% won't do, which is learning how to do it.

That makes things a lot easier, but to climb to the top you are going to have to do things differently from everybody else, which means you must first consciously decide that you want to climb to the top.

The only way to get to the top 1% is to spend your time differently from everybody else.

Now, there is never enough time in the day to be a top 1% applicant in every sector in banking and finance.

So by logical reasoning, the only way to get into the top 1% of applicants and to be among the 1% who climb to the top, you will need to manage that time well.

The only feasible action is to become a master of a particular sector in banking and finance and expand your horizons on your journey to the top.

Here is the mistake I made, and 99% make: they know they want to work in banking and finance, but they don't know where, so they make loads of generic applications and get rejection after rejection.

Their plan only stretches as far as getting the job, so many don't make it past the first few months.

As they are making so many applications, they write similar answers for all the different roles for which they are applying and get nowhere.

Influence Tool 10
Think beyond just getting the job

The 1% way is to spend time figuring out what you are passionate about and what you will be great at within banking and finance and commit to doing whatever it takes to be the best candidate for your chosen sub-sector in banking and finance.

One thing all humans have in common is that we all have the same amount of time in the day. That's obvious. But what is not so obvious is why some achieve an awful lot in that day, while others achieve nothing day after day.

It is how you spend your time that makes all the difference. We can give ourselves the illusion that we are investing our time wisely, but we can only measure if we are spending our time wisely if we know what outcome we are going for.

Influence Tool 11
Find ways to do two things at the same time, e.g. listen to self-development CDs while you drive

Simple, I know. But all my experience tells me that most people pick random stuff to do, based upon advice from those who have not achieved the result they are looking for, without clearly defining what they are going for and wonder why they are not feeling fulfilled in life.

You see, focus has this amazing knock-on effect.

What is the power that brothers Emanuel and Meyer Lehman tap into? Or later, Emanuel's son, Philip Lehman?

When the brothers created the investment bank Lehman Brothers, it served as a role model for dozens, emulated by Goldman Sachs, Bear Stearns, Drexel Burcham to name a few.

Today there is a long list of Jewish names on the front doors of leading investment firms, essentially all of whom followed the Lehmans' model.

As the role model for Jewish financial institutions, Emanuel Lehman and his son Philip will be held in high regard forever. But when asked about Philip Lehman, it was said, 'At anything he did, Philip had to win'.

The Lehmans knew specifically and precisely what the goal was: to create the model for Jewish financial institutions.

What is the power that a JP Morgan taps into when he becomes the modern day equivalent of a central bank?

What does Michael Bloomberg do differently when he creates more wealth in a year than the combined annual salary of most investment bankers?

How does William Paterson persuade the King of England to make his company the banker for the government and gain the right to literally print money?

Why does Mike Harris see opportunity when all others see impossibility?

What is it that Warren Buffett planned when he tried to work for free after being rejected by Benjamin Graham?

How did B C Forbes become the first journalist in the exclusive Wall Street club?

I believe that the Lehmans and all the other greats in banking and finance discussed in this book have tapped into the power of something called the 'Reticular Activating System' (RAS).

You see, here is the true power of focus. We have this mechanism in our brain called the Reticular Activating System. Although it sounds complicated to non-psychologists or non-scientists, its implications are very simple.

The RAS is the part of our brain that determines what our conscious mind focuses on and deletes.

In any one moment there are an infinite number of things that one can focus on and the conscious mind can only handle so many.

So in order to stay sane, we need to delete information from our conscious mind and leave it in our subconscious mind.

For example, have you ever bought a new car or item of clothing and then noticed that lots of other people have the same car or item of clothing all of a sudden?

Did they have that before your purchase or did everybody suddenly purchase it at the same time?

The answer is you started to notice it as your RAS made noticing it a part of your conscious mind.

It was there all along, but you chose not to focus on it before. This is how our brains work.

When we have focus, we interpret all information around us through its meaning to our area of focus.

When we meet people, we interpret what they say through our RAS; when we watch television we interpret it differently; depending on how we have tuned our RAS, everything changes.

This is why some are blind to opportunity and others are open.

What do you think you might see differently on a day to day basis if you trained your brain to think like Philip Lehman?

What if you believed that in anything you do you have to win?

You see, there is no such thing as failure, only quitters. If you see the first rejection as failure, then you are a quitter, not a failure. Quitters give up because their brain sees rejection; Philip sees a new experience that takes him one step closer to winning.

Influence Tool 12
Failing is your friend, quitting is your enemy

There is no question of the end goal – he has to win, it is a question of when. With every rejection, there is a vital bit of information that you can train your RAS to interpret as a lesson.

It is just disguised as rejection. It is part of the winning plan, it has taken Philip one step closer to creating his empire, there is no choice, but to win.

What if you decided that you were going to focus all your efforts into getting a trading role at Goldman Sachs?

What if, like Sidney Weinberg, one of the youngest partners in Goldman Sachs' history, who started as an assistant porter (we will discuss more on Sidney Weinberg later in this chapter), you saw each rejection as one step closer to partner at Goldman Sachs, even if your starting point was as an assistant porter?

Sidney Weinberg followed the first three tools of influence: he knew where he was starting out, he knew where he was going and actually had a map for how to climb from porter to partner, called his success formula.

What if you channelled everything you had into achieving that goal and you had to win? What if you changed the way your brain is hard-wired and instead asked the question "How long will it take until I win?" instead of "Will I fail or succeed?" Do you think this might change the way you see opportunity, or rejection?

We see things differently when we have focus. So now, if you decide to channel your brain into a particular sector in banking and finance, all of a sudden you will see new opportunity all around you, you will train your brain to focus on different actions, you will see how to become the ideal candidate and start to meet people in your field. You won't be studying, you will study with a purpose.

There is a huge difference between passively reading a book and reading it with a goal of what you want to get out of the book. This is the RAS in action.

Influence Tool 13
Learn something new towards your area of focus every day

It is a very powerful tool when used consciously.

You have a choice: either you decide to consciously take control of your brain, or you are controlled by another person's vision.

There is no in-between; you are either conscious or the victim of somebody else's conscious effort.

Focus is like a laser beam that deletes all irrelevant information and guides you like Adam Smith's invisible hand to the information you need to climb to the top in your field.

Every conversation becomes useful, every day becomes useful, your time becomes more productive.

So your first task is to figure out what sector in banking and finance is your area of focused effort.

One of the first things I do with students of my Banking and Finance Professional Program, after spending some time getting their mind in the right place to climb to the top, is select an area of focus from ten main sectors in banking and finance.

At the end of this chapter I give a quick description of ten sectors you may choose to narrow your focus down to, so we can lay your plan to climb to the top in banking and finance.

Once focused, you are ready for Influence Tool 14.

Influence Tool 14
Set big, fat, hairy goals

Let me ask you a quick question: What do Virgin, Apple, Dell and Microsoft all have in common?

The answer is they were all started during a recession by people aged under 25 with big goals that everyone else thought were crazy.

I remember sitting behind eight trading screens on the trading floor at investment bank KBC Peel Hunt when the CEO at the time, Tim Cockroft, announced his departure.

At the time, I was making a market in about 200 alternative investment market equities, and my trading partner was at lunch.

The next day a very young-looking corporate financier called Simon Hayes stepped in as CEO. I remember my thoughts at the time...

How did he get there?

What did he do differently from all the others?

How did he do it so young?

This really sparked an interest in me and the very next week I stepped out of my comfort zone, knocked on his door and told him why I wanted to follow in his footsteps and move into corporate finance...a big, fat, hairy statement, I know.

At the time, I didn't know what made me do it, but something inside me told me that to follow in the footsteps of those who are achieving the results you want to achieve was the right thing to do.

My observation after obsessing over the subject of achievement in banking and finance is that all top achievers do things differently from the rest. They all see opportunity while others see fear.

Influence Tool 15
Train your brain to see opportunity

You see, when I spoke with Simon Hayes, his age was not an issue. He seemed ultra-confident and ultra-ambitious. But where did that come from?

How about Sidney Weinberg, the father of the modern Goldman Sachs as we know it today, mentioned earlier? Weinberg stepped up from nothing to partner in his thirties.

With only an eighth-grade education, he began his business career at 15. His first job was holding people's places in bank run queues for $5 a spot.

Next, he managed to gain entrance into a Wall Street skyscraper. Working his way from bottom to top, he knocked confidently on the door of 24 Wall Street companies asking for work (when was the last time anybody did that?).

After receiving 24 rejections, he was hired by Goldman Sachs to assist the porter; by the age of 37 he was made a partner ahead of others senior to him and built Goldmans' investment banking division into what it is today.

Weinberg said because of his personality, hard work, good health, integrity, character and an eagerness to go above and beyond what was required, he climbed faster than anybody else. His 'personal success formula' would later become standard for investment bankers from his time until the present.

Influence Tool 16
Have a success formula that involves investing in new skills on a weekly basis

He was the role model for modern day investment bankers, and in that sense played a key role in how modern day corporate finance evolved.

Influence Tool 17
Find your role model

But why was he willing to take that first job as a porter? I believe he took it for the same reason that I took my first job as a tea boy at stockbrokers TD Waterhouse: because he had a plan with a big, fat, hairy goal, and assistant porter at Goldman Sachs was the first step in achieving his big, fat, hairy goal.

Influence Tool 18
Better to start at the bottom of your area of focus than in the middle of a role you are not passionate about. Think long term over short term gains

Later, Weinberg served on as many as 31 corporate boards at a single time including Goldman Sachs, Ford Motors, General Electric and General Foods to mention a few.

I have found that the very thing holding students and graduates back has nothing to do with the lack of good grades, top education or the fact that they are an international student with no work experience, but a lack of big, fat, hairy goals.

Once you are focused and you have decided in which sector you want to climb to the top, you will need to give yourself a big, fat, hairy goal early on.

A big, fat, hairy goal is one that people think you are crazy for even believing.

It is the one that drives the 'Don't be ridiculous' response from most people.

If people don't look at you and say you're an idiot, then it is not big enough, not fat enough and not hairy enough.

Mike Harris, the founder of the first telephone bank, First Direct, and the founder of the first internet-only bank, Egg, (in fact three multi-billion pound businesses) told me before I sat down to write this book, "Either revolutionise, reform, transform or don't do it."

This comes from a multi-millionaire in banking and finance; perhaps we have something to learn.

What big, fat, hairy goal did JP Morgan have? Unlike presidents and royalty who have power bestowed upon them, John Pierpont (JP) Morgan carried his larger than life status by sheer will.

Sure, he had a head start from his father, international banker Julius Morgan, but JP was the one who truly immortalised the House of Morgan by forming America's first billion dollar corporation in 1901 and, as 'big daddy', rescuing the economy from the grips of the 1907 Panic. While JP Morgan has his share of critics who question his intentions, you can bet he had a big, fat, hairy goal or two in him to be the first person who became the modern day equivalent of a central bank.

When writing your goals, never underestimate what you can achieve. If you do, you are like everybody else, and everybody else will not climb to the top in banking and finance.

When I undertook a university road show presenting at over 200 different universities, I would sometimes get criticism, saying that I was giving false hopes to those who have no chance.

But I do not believe that; this is them projecting their limited thinking on others because it is not within their reality. Remember these are the same people who are happy to give advice about how to achieve at the level they have currently achieved.

I suggest that, when this happens, you let their limited beliefs inspire you to action. When you hear something like that, don't you want to prove those people wrong?

I have found that when people say 'you can't', it is a great driver for me to prove them wrong.

> ## Influence Tool 19
> ### *Search for the good in everything*

There can be huge strength in ego when channelled in the right direction. We all have ego, we can use it to destroy us or inspire us to action.

Take Elias Jackson Baldwin, the founder of one of the earliest alternative stock exchanges, The Pacific Stock Exchange.

Baldwin started his stock exchange after being refused entry into The California Stock Exchange.

"By gad, I ain't been licked," Baldwin said on more than one occasion. Aggravated and annoyed, he vowed revenge and it came in the form of the Pacific Stock Exchange.

He proceeded to move more than 20 prestigious local members away from the other exchange to his.

Baldwin left his legacy based upon this initial moment of rejection, in order to bring finance to the local level when it was needed to build America's natural resource production.

With big, fat, hairy goals, history has shown that if anybody is 100% committed to a decision they can always find a way.

"I started with nothing, and I have been in every kind of business and succeeded in all...you know, I think if a man is determined he can do anything. I was determined." Elias Jackson Baldwin

My big, fat, hairy goal:

"I want to reform banking."

The week before writing this chapter, I was invited to Westminster to discuss the future of banking and finance with

MPs before meeting banking transformer Mike Harris to do some consultancy work. I was invited to a banking reform conference to present on monetary reform, after which I flew to Italy to write a book for the next generation of banking and finance leaders. The power of a big, fat, hairy, focused goal? Everything seems to come together when you know what you want.

Throughout this book, develop your big, fat, hairy banking and finance goal, in fact let's do an exercise right now.

Exercise 2 - Big, fat, hairy goal setting

Step 1

Take a piece of paper and write down the answers to the following questions:

1. **If you were watching your loved ones at your own funeral, what five things would you want them to say about you?**

2. **If you could not fail, what five things would you like to achieve in banking and finance?**

3. **What goal would be big enough, fat enough and hairy enough to make the people around you think that you are crazy, that you would love to achieve in banking and finance?**

4. **In order to achieve that big, fat, hairy goal what would you need to learn?**

5. **What skills would you need to master in order to achieve that big, fat, hairy goal?**

Step 2

Take two minutes to write a paragraph about what it would mean to you and the people you care about to achieve that big, fat, hairy goal.

continued ▶

Step 3

Draw a time line with about ten or more steps that would lead to that big, fat, hairy goal becoming a reality.

Step 4

Add a time period to each of the ten steps that you think you could make progress towards.

Step 5

Write down five things you could do in the next few days in order to move one step closer to the first of the ten steps.

Step 6

What one action could you take right now in order to commit you to taking one of those steps forward?

Now let's recap what we must do to lay our foundation for climbing to the top.

▼ **We must decide where we are committed to focused efforts**

▼ **We need to be more productive with our time**

▼ **We commit to a big, fat, hairy goal in our area of focus**

Once we are committed, in Chapter 3 we will investigate whether we are willing to do what it takes...

Knowledge Bite - The 10 main sectors in banking and finance

When a student or graduate enrolls on my Banking and Finance Professional Program, we give them an **endorsed and accredited** crash course in banking and finance to make sure they are aware of the main sectors in banking and finance.

On the course I break banking and finance up into ten main sectors.

influence your way to the **top** in **banking** and **finance**

Investment Banking

Investment banking is the traditional aspect of investment banks which involves helping customers raise funds in the capital markets and advising on mergers and acquisitions.

Other terms for the investment banking division include mergers and acquisitions (M&A) and corporate finance.

Investment banking includes the advisory, execution and deal-making activities likely to take place in a corporate finance environment.

Sales & Trading

One of the primary functions of an investment bank is buying and selling products, both on behalf of the bank's clients and also for the bank itself.

The broking and dealing division executes buy and sell orders, normally for private investors.

Market makers make prices in different financial markets by putting together buyers and sellers with some speculation on the direction of the market.

Structurers structure more or less bespoke financial products for clients.

Proprietary traders generate revenues through speculation with the institution's capital or credit.

Sales traders and institutional salespeople suggest new products and trading ideas to clients and find the best price for their ideas.

Asset Management

Asset management can refer to any form of fund management, wealth management, money management, portfolio management, investment management and other names that are used interchangeably.

Asset management is the professional management of various financial products (shares, bonds, etc.) and other assets (e.g. property, private equity), to meet specified investment goals for the benefit of the investors.

Investors may be institutions (insurance companies, pension funds, corporations etc.) or private investors (both directly via investment contracts and more commonly via collective investment schemes e.g. mutual funds, OIECS).

Commercial, Corporate & Retail Banking

A retail bank is basically a normal high-street bank, often called 'commercial' to distinguish it from an investment bank. Its clients are ordinary retail customers like you and me.

Some have used the term 'commercial bank' to refer to banks which focus mainly on companies, otherwise known as corporate banking.

Retail banking focuses on deposits, loans and the sale of other financial products to smaller customers and companies.

Corporate banks deal mostly with the deposits and loans from corporations and large businesses.

Research & Analysis

Research analysts analyse different areas of the institution, financial products and the institution's clients.

Working in asset management, investment banking and various other types of financial institutions, the research division reviews companies, financial products and writes reports about their prospects, often with 'buy' or 'sell' ratings.

While the research division generates no revenue, its resources are used to assist traders in trading, the salesforce in suggesting ideas to customers, and investment bankers by publishing reports on their clients.

Back & Middle Office

Each financial institution has people who bring in revenue, assist in bringing in revenue or provide an environment for those who bring in revenue to function. People working in Back & Middle Office (also known as operations), unlike front office, don't liaise with customers to generate revenues and profits for the financial institution. Operations run as a support function to the front office (the revenue-generating activities).

Middle Office includes activities like compliance, risk management and marketing, while Back Office includes activities like operations, technology, human resources and finance.

Insurance

Insurance companies, in return for assuming an insurance risk, charge a premium. They hope that their premium income will exceed the money they have to pay to those with legitimate insurance claims. If an insurance company feels that the risks it runs are too great, it can pass some of them on to a second company, the process known as reinsurance.

Insurance money can be invested by the insurance company and therefore makes up a significant part of the money invested with asset managers.

Accounting & Tax

As the collectors and interpreters of financial information, accountants develop comprehensive knowledge of virtually all business functions and relationships with key decision makers.

Managerial accounting involves the identification, measurement, accumulation, analysis, preparation, interpretation and communication of financial information used by management to plan, evaluate, control and assure the appropriate use of its resources.

Financial accounting, on the other hand, is a field that deals with the financial accounting process in the preparation of financial reports, such as daily balance sheets and quarterly or yearly income statements that help to answer questions such as 'What is the financial position of the firm on a given day?' and 'How well did the firm do during a given period?'

Within these main areas of accounting exists a variety of custom tailored sub-types that address specific needs such as auditing, taxation and consulting.

Consulting

A niche area of banking and finance is the consultancy industry. All consultancies have their own specialisms. The banking and finance sector uses consultants for a range of activities.

Consultants think, analyse, brainstorm, cajole and challenge good financial institutions to become even better by adopting new ideas.

Financial consultants provide financial advice to corporations and money managers. The essence of management consulting in banking and finance is to help a financial institution obtain information and advice which leads to real and lasting solutions of a problem.

Law in Banking and Finance

The financial services industry is built on trust; customers must know their best interests are being protected. In many parts of the industry, trust has been supplemented by lots of government regulation aimed at protecting customers, investors and the economy.

Legal professionals tend to work directly in banking and finance as corporate financiers, advising on corporate law or compliance.

The compliance department ensures that internal controls and regulatory processes are carried out.

There are a great many other regulations that banks and insurers need to apply to their operations. These include anti money-laundering regulations, data protection rules, general duty of care, banking code, treating customers fairly etc.

CHAPTER THREE

Be Willing To Do It

influence
your way to the
top in banking
and finance

Influence Tool 20
Be ready for criticism

The more you achieve, the more problems you will face.

The higher you climb, the more criticism people will want to throw at you. Are you willing to do it?

To climb to the top will take conviction. You will encounter obstacles. I mean let's face it, one of the top jobs is prime minister or president of a country. Think of the problems you would face in that job.

No matter what you do, half of your country is going to hate you and try to tear you down.

If you want to climb to the top and you also want to win everybody's approval as you climb, you are in for trouble and a big internal conflict.

If it was easy, everyone would do it, but what keeps you motivated in those times of overwhelming problems?

The only thing that will keep you going is your passion, your mission and your reasons for doing it in the first place.

They need to be far bigger than anything else. My mission to implement a monetary reform as part of my ultimate mission to reform banking is a classic example of mission being bigger than any criticism and need for approval.

The burning desire to do what I know is right for the world is bigger than anything else.

All my adult life, I have been involved in banking and finance; I even met my wife in a bank while opening a business bank account.

People misinterpret my mission all the time.

Capitalists sometimes think I am a radical anti-capitalist reformer, even though I run three businesses in banking and finance.

Anti-capitalists cannot believe that I could be a part of the banking sector and claim to be a monetary reformer.

Sceptics accuse me of reforming in order to benefit financially for self-interest.

Bankers often think that I am anti-debt or other crazy things as I explain the inherent flaws in our current monetary and financial system.

Sometimes students who don't know me accuse me of being a scam as I run a business that charges students for training. They think it should be free for some reason!

Perhaps one day I will turn this into a charity, but my experience tells me that people do not appreciate things that are free and you do people a disservice when they are not taught the lesson of having to work hard and put their hard-earned money up to truly appreciate it and get the results they need. I learnt this lesson when I worked hard to pay for the training I needed to fulfill my mission.

Anyway, the truth is I stand for a banking system that incorporates all the functionality of the current financial system under a stable monetary system.

A system where money is created for the good of the public with a value-focused and empowered next generation of banking and finance leaders who are self-responsible, motivated, passionate and socially responsible.

This seems too strange for some to understand though, but their criticism cannot hold back my passion and belief of what is the right thing to do for the world.

My goal is not to please the critics, it is to do what I know in my soul is the right thing for society.

I will save this one for another book. If the subject of how our current banking system is unsustainable and harmful to our nation is something that interests you, you can watch one of my keynote presentations at www.simondixon.org

This type of criticism serves as a personal example of what happens the bigger your passion and mission becomes.

So once you know what you want, you have to ask the question, "Am I willing to do it?"

Experience tells me that anybody who harnesses some of the tools I outline in this book is capable of a bigger mission than they give themselves credit for.

Knowing that the more you achieve the more criticism you will get, you will need to make a true decision about whether you are willing to do it or not.

Once you know your outcome, you have decided that modelling success from the top provides the best map, you are focused, you are going to invest your time more wisely than anybody else, you have set your big, fat, hairy banking and finance goals, the other missing ingredient is to decide.

Most people rarely make decisions. I was taught a long time ago that a true decision is to cut off any other possibility. A true decision means that you either find a way or make a way.

Influence Tool 21
Find a way, or make a way

One of my Banking and Finance Professional Program graduates is a true inspiration for all.

Cecilia was studying biochemistry after moving to the UK from China. Having realised that her true passion lay in corporate finance, she set about making her dream become a reality.

Despite having every reason not to succeed, she set about turning herself into the perfect candidate.

She began by figuring out what the perfect corporate financier looked like and then spent a year moulding herself into the perfect corporate financier.

Cecilia understood that combining her ability to bring in new business as well as financial understanding were equally important. So immediately she wanted to work on her communication so she could work with the best.

She delivered an irresistible value proposition to one of my companies that was too good to refuse, landing herself some work experience. You could call it a 'Mafia Offer' that I could not refuse.

I work with a handful of pre-selected students and graduates on what I call my Platinum Plus Partnership, where one of the first things we do is construct a Mafia Offer for the people with whom they want to connect and lay out a plan for how to reach them.

Cecilia made herself indispensable in whatever she did, and we were very sad to lose her when she left to study for her Masters in corporate finance, run the Investment Society and get her relevant work experience.

Her goal behind the work experience was to step outside of her comfort zone and face her fears head on, so she took every opportunity to speak with people over the phone and build her confidence.

***

Influence Tool 22
Work on your feared things first

***

Cecilia started to sit her relevant professional qualifications in her free time.

Cecilia did not let the huge financial commitment of a Masters stop her; she started to fund her studies by learning how to trade the financial markets after working with my trading consultancy company and completing my Professional Trader Program.

Shortly after, she pitched her way to her first internship in private equity. A few months later, she called me to let me know she was flying off to Wall Street, having secured an offer in corporate finance during the peak of the financial crisis.

***

Influence Tool 23
Invest in the relevant training for your ideal role - don't wait for the company to pay for it

***

Cecilia had everything against her in the traditional sense. When I first met her she was very shy, quiet and not confident in her English. She had the wrong degree, visa problems and suffered many rejections along the way as well as financial difficulties.

But she had something much bigger than any setback: she had made a decision to make it in corporate finance. There was no alternative. Her determination shone through and allowed her to overcome all hurdles.

She had the Philip Lehman mindset – she had to win.

Influence Tool 24
Stay committed to your decisions

Nothing was going to stop her. She truly harnessed the power of all the tools outlined in this book and is living proof that when you are determined enough and focused enough with the correct map there is always a way.

Influence Tool 25
Tell everyone what you have decided to do and do it

I have found that a great tool to make you follow through on your decisions is to tell the world of your intentions. Sure, you risk looking like an idiot and everyone telling you that you can't do it, but allow that to motivate you to action.

An example of this principle in action is the book you are reading right now. I made a decision that I wanted to write a book to inspire students and graduates to climb to the top in banking and finance.

Once the decision had been made, I took action and steps to make sure it became a reality. I told everyone on television that I was the author of the book before it was finished.

Now having thousands of students and graduates contacting me to purchase the book was leverage enough to make it a reality.

Shortly after the announcement, I freed up my diary, found the time and flew to Italy with my wife to make the book happen.

I figured out how to write a book and just did it. I knew nothing about writing books, getting books published or how to do it. I made a decision, told everybody about that decision and then just figured out the rest.

Influence Tool 26
After making a decision, do something that commits you immediately

How often do you make decisions?

99% of people decide upon things they 'should' do, but rarely make a decision.

Everybody knows what it is like when you truly make a decision, when you say, "No more" or "That's it" or "I have had enough" and immediately follow it up with action.

The only decisions that happen are the ones we 'must' do. If you must do it, you find a way or make a way.

So make a decision about something right now and, while you are passionate about it, take one small action that commits you towards its achievement.

I went to a seminar where we had to walk on burning coal in order to demonstrate what the mind was capable of doing when used correctly.

Once you take that first step, you take the next twenty steps; all you needed to do was make the decision to take the first step. It was a powerful experience that I recommend to anybody.

You cannot imagine what you are capable of doing once you decide.

What have you decided about your banking and finance career?

When students and graduates complete my Banking and Finance Professional Program we make decisions about what type of financial institution we are going to work for and lay out the plan for any market.

Once the decision has been made, there are several things that must follow to make it a reality.

You must be willing to step outside of your comfort zone consistently and you must understand that failure and rejection are inevitable, predictable and guaranteed ingredients on your journey to the top.

What makes the difference is the meaning you attach to the rejection and failure.

The top 1% interpret rejection and failure differently from the other 99%. Are you willing to experience the rejection that is inevitable the higher you climb?

Influence Tool 27
Become a sponge for information

For two months I had been getting up at five in the morning and going home at ten at night, to and from my office at 101 Deansgate, Manchester.

My desk was overlooking a separate glass-doored office where the CEO of TD Waterhouse frequently strolled in and out from meeting to meeting.

I could see through the office and would often imagine and wonder about his journey to CEO.

What sequence of events led to him climbing to the top?

I was always inspired by other people's success and would ask them questions at every available opportunity, soaking up information like a sponge.

I wanted to know how everything on the dealing floor worked, what everybody did and anything I could get my hands on.

The office floor was open plan and I was next to the dealers who would ring orders through to the market makers, normally in London.

As I was on a temping contract, obviously the company would not help me to undertake my exams, so I would often stay behind afterwards, seeking out any overtime, and if there was no overtime I would just stay behind and study for my exams to make me an FSA approved person and watch others as they dealt on the international markets.

I would listen for the language they used, write it down and go home and research what it meant. I built most of my knowledge this way as I did not undertake any graduate scheme training or anything like that.

Everything was learning by observing, then eventually doing.

Influence Tool 28
Do ten times more for others than you ask in return

My goal was simple: I wanted to be a stockbroker and I wanted to get on the phones with the dealers and start to build my connections.

My strategy was simple: do more than everyone else, work harder than everyone else, never complain, never use excuses, soak up all the information around me, study for my exams and ask for a job on the dealing desk after proving my value.

But more important than all that, I had a mentor who guided me.

I sought out those who loved what they do and would always freely offer great value to them until they agreed to help.

I made a habit of doing ten times more for them than I ever asked in return.

My mentor owned his own financial advisory practice in Leeds and he taught me early on that the key to success is adding value.

He taught me to always give at least ten times more than you ask for; he taught me that we get paid the amount of value that we are currently adding and that if we are not getting paid as much as we want, it is because we are not giving enough.

A principle that has served me well to this day.

One evening, I left work a little earlier than normal as I had arranged a meeting with my mentor to discuss how I could get promoted from my current role as tea boy and general admin worker to getting on the dealing desk with all the other stockbrokers.

I had already been entrusted with responsibility outside of my role and was given more and more customer service duty, but my mission was to get on the dealing floor.

Influence Tool 29
Do more than your mentor tells you to do

My mentor had told me to read a book by an author called Les Brown, entitled Live Your Dream. I did one better – I bought the tape pack and the book and listened to it several times before our meeting. Whenever somebody asks me to do something, I have an obsessive compulsion to over-deliver and go that step further so I am fully prepared.

As we sat down for dinner, he told me that I was to introduce myself to the director the following morning. Terrified by the sight of the big glass doors near my desk, I forecasted what my mentor was going to say next; having already read the Les Brown book several times over, I knew how he got his first big break.

Influence Tool 30
Always step outside of your comfort zone and raise the bar

At this point I had reached what is known as a 'comfort zone'.

A comfort zone is the point at which we become comfortable in our situation.

I had been doing the job for two months now, the first hurdle of getting my foot in the door was over, I was now becoming used to hanging around in the dealing room and my mentor told me that it was time to step outside of my comfort zone.

The strange thing about comfort zones is that in seeking the comfortable, safe and secure feeling we very often crave, we always reach a point of internal conflict where we no longer feel like we are growing. The feeling of uncertainty that we experience when we are growing and trying new things is replaced by an equally uncomfortable feeling of boredom as we experience a lack of growth.

As humans we often seek some form of variety in other ways in order to satisfy our craving for uncertainty.

If everything in our world were certain, there would be no surprises, no new experiences, no juice.

What complicated creatures we humans can be.

The funny thing about life is that all achievement occurs outside of the comfort zone that we so often try to avoid.

If I have learnt one thing over the years, it is that those top 1% have embraced the feeling of stepping outside of their comfort zone and consistently try new things with uncertain results.

If we only do things we are comfortable with, we never experience new things and life becomes dull, unfulfilling and we never grow.

Once you become consciously aware of this, you learn how to harness the feeling; you just feel the fear and do it anyway.

In fact, Susan Jeffers wrote a whole book on this subject entitled Feel The Fear And Do It Anyway. I was discussing this book recently with Simon Woodroffe, one of the VCs from the TV show Dragons' Den and he said, "The title says it all."

I digress; it was time for me to step outside of my comfort zone and do what nobody else was doing.

Remember, if you want to be where the 1% are, do like them; but the 1% do things differently, so like Les Brown described in his book, I leapt into the director's office the very next morning and introduced myself to him as instructed by my mentor.

Influence Tool 31
Make an impression wherever you go

After introducing myself to the director, I let him know that I was looking for a job in stockbroking.

The funny thing was that the story I was creating in my head about what might happen when I knocked on the door was the opposite of what actually happened when he told me to take a seat and proceeded to interview me.

To cut a long story short, he thought that having been with the firm for only two months, it would be unfair on those who had been waiting in line patiently for years, and besides, he said that there were currently 'no jobs'.

While I was willing to wait, I thought to myself 'there has got to be a better way', so I reported back to my mentor and he told me to refer to the book for the next steps.

He reminded me how the story goes and demanded that I go and knock on the director's door the very next day and try again.

Influence Tool 32
Expect the best, but prepare for the worst

Nervously, I awaited the CEO's arrival the next day.

I made it a habit to be one of the first to arrive every morning, so after he arrived I gave him a few minutes to settle in and marched over to the big glass doors once again.

This time nerves got the better of me and I walked straight past the doors and to the bathroom to calm my nerves.

Splashing some water on my face and trying to use the hand dryer to dry the collar of my shirt, I proceeded to whip myself up into a frenzy.

Making my way over to the glass doors again, I knocked and introduced myself to the director as if I had never seen him before and explained that I wanted to be a stockbroker.

Confused, he responded as if to say, 'Didn't we have this very same conversation yesterday?' to which I responded jokingly that I was just checking that nobody had quit since yesterday.

Influence Tool 33
Seek first to understand, then be understood

With a confused look on his face, it gave me an opportunity to give him more reasons why I was, in fact, the person he needed to work on the stockbroking dealing desk.

You see, during our interview the previous day I was given the opportunity to ask him what makes for a great stockbroker and now, armed with this knowledge, I was able to explain how I was the ideal candidate in his words which got his attention a lot more than my interview yesterday.

The conversation seemed to be going well until the phone rang and he hurried me out of the office, signalling that he was too busy to continue.

I thanked him for his time and left him to his phone call.

Reporting back to my mentor that evening and explaining what had happened, he told me to do it again the next day.

Now this is the point where most will quit and continue doing things as everybody else does because another rejection and the thought of knocking on the door again was causing some serious disturbance to my comfort zone.

Influence Tool 34
Expect 12 rejections until a 'cold' deal is completed

To say that this was a leap outside of my comfort zone was an understatement, but one of my mentors, Tony Robbins, is famous for saying, "It is in our moments of decision that our destiny is shaped."

So the very next morning I awaited the CEO's arrival and proceeded to the gents to calm my overpowering nerves.

I sucked it up, felt the fear and did it anyway. I leapt into the office confidently and introduced myself as if I had never seen him before, stating that I wanted to be a stockbroker.

He responded angrily with a raised voice that there were no jobs, nobody had quit since yesterday, he knew my name was Simon Dixon, he knew I wanted to be a stockbroker, as if to say, 'What do you want?'

With a humorous tone, I responded by asking him if anybody on the stockbroking desk had died since yesterday.

In disbelief, he rolled over in fits of laughter and I figured that now was as good a time as any to make my dreams a reality.

Influence Tool 35
Promise results, then deliver

I remembered our first conversation in which he had told me that stockbrokers are willing to take rejection and the best bring in new business all the time. I quickly reminded him of his words and asked him, "If I use the determination that I am showing with you with all of the clients I work with, do you think this might be something that would be useful on the dealing desk?"

I then made him a promise that if he gave me the opportunity next week to start as a stockbroker and I could not bring in more business than the equivalent of what he had paid me, then I would return to my old role.

I made it a 'no brainer' for him to accept. You see there are two forces that make hiring you a 'no brainer'. When you can deliver results in advance through a clear demonstration and when you can guarantee more value than they have to pay you in wages... combine these two forces and you have a Mafia Offer.

If you have already proved that you are not just words and, in fact, you can deliver results and you guarantee more value than you get paid, then hiring you is the obvious rational thing to do.

I left him with no choice, and he hired me as a stockbroker on the dealing desk the very next week.

Influence Tool 36
See opportunities where others see rejections

Now I don't know if you have ever experienced a situation in which you have achieved something that you have wanted so badly for so long and you start to freak out because you never really imagined it would happen that quickly.

Well, all of a sudden I was overwhelmed with fear. I had made a big promise and needed to deliver.

That very same weekend I wondered what I was going to do to bring in some new business and set my RAS in motion.

That night I leapt out of bed with a plan. I quickly ruffled through my drawers in order to find some paperwork, hoping and praying that I had not thrown it away.

As I searched through the mess in my drawer, halfway down I found piles of multi-coloured paper with the logos of over 100 different broking houses, investment banks and investment institutions printed on them.

It was the pile of rejection letters from my days when I was making multiple applications and sending CVs to every financial institution I could find.

I decided that these were no longer rejection letters, but were opportunities.

I devised a plan to call up the contact name on each of the rejection letters, asking to be put through to the broking department as I now worked on the dealing desk for TD Waterhouse and wanted to discuss new business and working together.

To cut a long story short, I delivered. I brought in record levels of new business and this is one of the very defining moments in my life that led to the fulfillment of my dreams that I live today.

I think the true value in this story is that through our RAS we have the choice to see anything how we choose to see it.

Even rejection letters can be opportunity if you look at them with different eyes.

The meaning that we give to things can actually alter the results that we achieve.

Influence Tool 37
Be careful of the meaning you attach to life circumstances

At the time of writing we are experiencing one of the worst financial crises and recessions in decades.

I have found that the very thing holding students and graduates back right now is simply the meaning that they attach to the current market.

In private equity our job is to see things differently from everyone else.

The investments that I look for at present are companies that do not understand the opportunity that is available to them right now through technological advance.

I mean, never in history have we had access to our own television channel (You Tube), our own distribution network of over half a billion users (Facebook), the ability to have our message reach everyone's pockets (through iPhones and Blackberries), access to our own publishing company (through iPad and Amazon), the ability to set up, at virtually zero cost for three people to be able to do the work of 300 people without an office and access to a global market with the click of a few buttons and a small budget (with Google).

And this is meant to be a hard time?

What an opportunity for those who can train their RAS.

As long as businesses continue to do things the old way, there will always be a market for me to see things the other way and thrive.

As long as students and graduates try old traditional methods to secure a top-paying career in banking and finance, there will always be an opportunity for others to see things another way and climb to the top.

Students and graduates who are struggling right now are stuck in the old ways and not adjusting to change.

Old-thinking students and graduates are using old strategies like 'get as educated as you can and then apply online for graduate schemes'.

This will lead to the same results as everybody else – a select few will get the job, but most will get rejected.

However, as we have seen, these rejections are actually part of the plan, depending on your beliefs and the meaning you give them.

Circumstances do not dictate what happens to us. The meaning that we give the circumstances does.

This tough market can be unfortunate or it can be the biggest opportunity ever.

Influence Tool 38
Give a meaning to everything that serves you rather than disempowers you

What meaning you give a recession is your choice.

What is the dominant meaning that you give to negative situations? The meaning you give it will dictate your results right now.

Some experience the trauma (and something that I would never wish upon anybody) of being raped.

Some take that experience and fall apart. Others use this as a reason to never allow this to happen to anybody ever again and start a crusade to change the world.

What is the difference?

The meaning you give it. The 'Why me?' versus 'How can I use this to serve me?' or 'What is the good in this?'

The meaning you attach to circumstances will dictate your ability to see the opportunity amongst the rough. So how can we control the meaning we give something? We ask ourselves intelligent questions that set our brain off on a new path of thought.

Influence Tool 39
Ask yourself better questions to change how you feel about anything

---

Try these for size…

▼ **What am I grateful for in my life right now?**

▼ **Who in my life do I love?**

▼ **Who loves me?**

▼ **Who in the world would kill to have my problems?**

▼ **What is Apple doing differently from General Motors?**

▼ **Who is getting jobs right now with less education and less going for them?**

▼ **What are they doing differently?**

▼ **What opportunity comes from the negative markets?**

▼ **What makes me different from all the other students and graduates in my class?**

Great questions, right? You might come up with a new meaning. In Chapter 5 we question our current beliefs and show how we are what we believe. Anything that can be conceived or believed can be achieved.

Understand what failure and rejection really are and decide whether you are willing to experience them to climb to the top.

So now we know that there is going to be criticism and rejection on our journey, we had better do this with something that we are truly passionate about...

CHAPTER FOUR

Be Passionate

Influence Tool 40
If it's worth doing, do it with passion

The message of this chapter is short and sweet.

Nothing will make you climb to the top faster or have more of a contribution to your success than following what you were born to do.

There is such a vast range of roles in banking and finance that anything short of what you are passionate about is the standard for climbing to the top in banking and finance.

It took nothing more than General Georges Doriot's passion for business to make him the founder of the first ever publicly listed risk capital firm that financed new businesses by selling new shares to the public.

American Research and Development Corporate was the firm that got the venture capital industry off the ground and marked a whole new opportunity for start-up entrepreneurs.

What drove Doriot to create a new industry that nobody before him would touch?

His undeniable passion about new business was more than the sceptics could throw at him. In fact he saw his investments as his own children.

"When you have a child, you don't ask what return you can expect...I want them to do outstandingly well in their field. And if they do, the rewards will come. But if a man is honest in his efforts and loyal and does not achieve a so-called good rate of return, I will stay with him...I am building men and companies."

He was so passionate about his investments that he would stick by them through thick and thin, once saying, "If a child is sick with 102 degrees fever, do you sell him?"

To get the venture capital industry moving took huge risks from Doriot. Without passion, how would he have found the guts, confidence, drive, patience, resourcefulness and total dedication that were essential when you read his story?

One of the founding principles behind Metal Monkey Private Equity is that when we make a new investment, it becomes part of our family, not just an investment to add to our portfolio.

It is not an emotionless investment, but a relationship where we have to go through a dating process to make sure we are compatible.

Our investments have always produced a tremendous return because we choose passion over profit. Of course the profit potential needs to be there, but without passion we decline.

When a new deal is placed on our doorstep, if we are not passionate then we don't really care about how much money it will make. Experience tells us that only working with investments in which we believe passionately has produced a tremendous return when we work as a family and benefit from each other's business experiences.

True wealth can only be earned when you love what you do.

We are going to spend most of our life at work, why on earth would we settle for something that we don't like doing?

In fact, replace the word 'work' with 'mission' and you are in the right frame of mind to make it to the top.

The only reason we would spend most of our life doing something we don't like doing would be because we have not integrated the 97 tools of influence into our life.

Focus can be useless if we are focusing in the wrong direction.

"Success comes not so much by forecasting as by doing the right thing at the right time and always being willing to keep one's course prudently protected." Roger Babson

Roger Babson understood the power of staying focused to your passion as he created and founded the Babson Statistical Organization Inc. that later became what we know today as Standard & Poors (S&P).

Roger Babson was inspired by Booker T Washington's claim that 'specialisation generates success'.

Babson was so passionate about the stock market analysis field that he created the first company dedicated to statistical research, even though it did not exist at the time. He created his own 'wheel' so to speak.

Over half a century of passionately staying focused to his mission, he created one of the first market newspapers, sparked an entire industry of non-institutional and retail analysis, invented his own stock market index and from it predicted the 1929 stock market crash.

His passion for statistical analysis lead him to the discovery that banks, investment houses and stock exchange firms needed statistics and indexes. This gave birth to a whole new industry in the financial arena.

What was the driving force behind Charles Merrill?

Charles Merrill was passionate about bringing Wall Street to Main Street.

He urged the small person with a spare thousand or two to invest in America's economy to start investing.

Through his passion, he was the first to do it on a grand scale, with huge long-term success as he created the powerhouse Merrill Lynch.

When Merrill knew he'd succeeded, he rejoiced, "America's industrial machine is owned at the grass roots, where it should be, and not in some mythical Wall Street."

His passion was so clear and he had a mission that was evident in his huge, innovative advertising campaigns with the purpose of making the ordinary citizen an investor, promoting the slogan 'Bring Wall Street to Main Street'.

So passionate was Charles Merrill that nothing could stop him as he filled an all-important role in the evolution of modern finance.

In the 19th century, it looked as if capitalism might mainly enrich a small elite group. But Charles Merrill's passion arrived at a time when the little man (not yet the little woman) would flourish into a thriving middle class.

He truly brought Wall Street to Main Street in a fashion that has lived on for decades after him.

▼ **So what is that thing that attracted you into banking and finance in the first place?**

▼ **What really annoys you?**

▼ **What is that thing that gets you out of bed in the morning?**

▼ **What area are you going to have an impact on?**

Find your passion early and the first job, the first promotion and the path to CEO takes care of itself as you move forward with your passion, your mission and your true purpose every day.

A word of warning though: setting a focused goal around your passion is the key to success, but if you don't believe you can do it, you will not climb to the top. So what creates that belief?

CHAPTER FIVE

Believe You Can Do It

I had reached an all time low.

The security guard pulled me aside and asked for my ID.

I was in Waterloo station, it was 6am and fortunately it was relatively quiet, but the rush of people on their way to work was soon to come.

I had broken the law and it was my fault. There was nowhere to run and nowhere to hide.

I was so embarrassed and could only hang my head in shame.

But what seemed like an all time low at the time turned out to be a key turning point in my life, one that took an interesting turn, one that was the pinnacle of a series of events and decisions that had taken me from living in a luxurious bachelor penthouse overlooking the River Thames in Chelsea Harbour to moving in with my wife-to-be because I could no longer afford the mortgage, selling my car and quitting my job, to raising finance with my business-angel-to-be, Peter Hargreaves – and the rest is history.

But it all began with an all time low...

It is interesting what effect a simple decision can have, but as stated earlier by one of my mentors, Anthony Robbins, "It is in our moments of decision that our destiny is shaped."

But what actually precedes a decision?

Influence Tool 41
Start with your beliefs

Before a decision is formed, a belief is shaped.

What you believe is possible will lead you to different decisions being made.

Different decisions being made lead you to a set of different actions.

This set of actions will lead you to an entirely different set of results.

Once you obtain these results, you have mental evidence to back up your belief.

Evidence to back up your belief, in turn, strengthens your original belief and the cycle repeats.

Influence Tool 42
The biggest challenge is to convince yourself you can do it

A stronger belief leads to different decisions. More decisions lead to more action. More action leads to more results. More results lead to more evidence to back up your ever-strengthening belief.

Like an ever-growing spiral, our belief of what is possible expands and expands.

This is the path to the top, this is the path to 1% status.

Whether consciously or subconsciously, this is the secret that the 1% harness.

This is why experienced people say things confidently, because they have evidence to back up their belief.

The interesting thing is what if we could simply start with the belief without the evidence and then develop the evidence to strengthen the belief? Could this fast-track our journey?

I have always admired Peter Hargreaves, so much so that I made it my mission to make him my business angel in one of my ventures.

Money and contacts aside, what happens to my belief when one of the most successful businessmen in the UK invests in my ideas?

It strengthens your belief tremendously as well as committing you towards making it a success. You don't want to be the person responsible for letting down one of the most successful business people in the UK.

And interestingly enough, where did Peter Hargreaves' confidence come from in the first place?

Influence Tool 43
Find out how great achievers started

Peter Hargreaves worked in audit and just decided to start a business from his bedroom.

He was in the same situation as many others, yet forward the clock 25 years and he has a net worth of over £500 million, a spot on The Times Rich List, hundreds of thousands of investors in his company that went public and joined the FTSE 250, a successful book, a leading wealth management institution and many angel investments like our training and consultancy company for students and graduates.

Although I have never discussed this with him, I believe it all started with the belief that he could do it, otherwise he would have stayed in audit like most of the others do.

He asked a few clients, if he started his business in wealth management would they use his company? Because one client said 'yes', this strengthened his belief and he did it.

After attracting more clients, his belief grew, his evidence to back up the belief grew and he attracted more and more businesses to his company; whether he knows it or not, this strengthens his belief.

This allows Peter Hargreaves to make confident decisions, it allows him to take bigger actions, these massive actions always lead to more results and, after producing results time and time again, his belief is strengthened rock-solid to the point where he makes decisions that have built him wealth worthy of inclusion on The Times Rich List.

What do you think happens to my belief when he invests in my ideas and writes about my ideas in his book?

Influence Tool 44
Pitch your ideas to everybody

This is the cycle of belief from which a mission is born. The biggest challenge is convincing yourself to believe that you can make a difference.

If you take no action because you don't believe, you never build up the evidence database and never build momentum.

So really, we are achieving what we truly believe is possible. We are simply limited by our beliefs.

Like Peter Hargreaves, all empires are built with a belief. The same with a JP Morgan, the same with a Mike Harris, the same with a Warren Buffett, the same with a John Templeton and the other tens of thousands of inspirational believers, decision makers, action takers, result getters who are available to inspire us all, who have all preceded us and made up the financial system as we know it today.

At the time of writing this book, our financial system is undergoing huge structural change as a result of our monetary system manifesting in the form of a financial crisis.

It is undergoing serious criticism from the public, but nonetheless it has been developed into a global engine through the gradual innovation of lots of small and large decisions.

These decisions all began with a belief that they could do it.

As we enter a new era we look to the next generation, the ones who set their big, fat, hairy goals, who had the strength of character to believe and set the spiral in motion.

What an opportunity the financial crisis can be for those who set their RAS in motion.

Some of you, unfortunately, will take the opposite road.

Some will allow the belief that achieving your big, fat, hairy goal is something that you can't do.

In our company, we have a name for these people. We call them 'wet blankets'. They also hang around with 'happiness thieves'. These are the people who suck the inspiration and motivation out of everybody around them. Almost every office and environment has a 'happiness thief'. The 'wet blankets' and the 'happiness thieves' spur each other on and destroy all inspiration around them.

You don't want to be a 'wet blanket' and you certainly don't want to be remembered as a 'happiness thief'.

Influence Tool 45
Be careful who you listen to

You will listen to the sceptics and when you don't believe you can do it, what hope have you got of stepping up and making a true decision to cut off any other possibility?

You may make a weak decision and take some half-hearted action, but the moment that any of your action leads to any form of inevitable rejection or negative result it will produce evidence in your brain that backs up your inner critic.

Influence Tool 46
Beware of the inner critic

The inner critic is an internal voice with which we are all familiar:

"See, you can't do it."

"Why did you even bother?"

"I told you so."

"Besides, you didn't go to the top uni."

"What makes you think you can do it?"

"You are a failure."

"Don't do that training. It might not work again. You might get excited for nothing, it must be a scam."

"Why did you fall for that again?"

"They are just trying to hype you up. It will work for them, but not me."

Sound familiar?

I was at a meeting with Simon Woodroffe recently who was sharing with me the conversations that he has with his inner critic.

Even though he has so much evidence to back up his belief that he is successful in business – by that I mean a spot as a VC on the hit TV show Dragons' Den, multiple successful multi-million pound businesses, a household brand to his name 'Yo Sushi' – he was describing these two characters that he speaks to, on his left and right shoulder.

One is the inner critic, the other is the dreamer.

One tells him he can't do it and searches for all the evidence in his past to back up that belief; the other tells him he can do it and searches for all the evidence to back up that belief from his past.

If you relate to this at all you will be aware of the internal game that our inner critic can play with us.

Thinking about it though, couldn't our mind search for evidence to back up any belief we wanted it to?

Influence Tool 47
Find the evidence that serves you

If we wanted evidence to back up the belief that 'money is evil', could we not search our brain for references to back up that belief and look for all the crooks, murderers and war crimes that stem from the quest for money?

Alternatively, how about the belief that 'money is good'? Could we find tremendous inspirational stories of the birth of microfinancing as it empowers more and more women from poverty into business? And how about the funding that allowed churches, synagogues, mosques, temples and other religious or spiritual buildings to be built in order to allow the public to come together and pray? How about leaders like Sir John Templeton who became a multi-billionaire fund manager and used his millions for all sorts of philanthropic good?

In an instant can we not search for fault in these great missions too?

Could we find evidence to back up the belief that microfinancing is simply profiting from the least privileged or that philanthropic business leaders are only donating to charity for self-interest and tax benefits?

Some question religion as being one big money-making scam.

We have the power to see things as we wish. The real question is which way will allow you to climb to the top if that is your goal in a way that is congruent with your ethics and beliefs.

Once we know what map of the world will serve us, can we simply choose to see things in a way that will serve us?

The answer is 'absolutely yes', and that is the difference between the 1% and the rest.

We can rationalise anything we choose.

I hold a belief that all humans are good and that they rationalise the good in everything they do when they take action.

I believe all humans are basically in a search for love.

How they find love may lead them to war, philanthropy, murder, saving the world and all sorts of conflicting actions.

But at the end of the day, we all want love and we all fear that we might not be good enough as we seek approval from others.

Do you see how we can all use our beliefs in order to destroy or serve?

Influence Tool 48
Stand at guard at the door to your mind

The key is to recognise that we have a choice and become conscious of our mind as we decide in which direction we want it to go, rather than unconscious like the 99% who hold beliefs, but those beliefs have been shaped from circumstance, environment, social conditioning, family, friends, the media and advertising.

You either choose your beliefs, or you adopt other people's beliefs.

If you have not chosen them consciously, then your beliefs are what you have been told they are. There is no in-between.

Anyway, back to the story where I broke the law...

After securing a career at KBC Peel Hunt in corporate finance, I was exposed to business owners, venture capitalists and CEOs seeking new investments and new finance.

When meeting these inspirational people, I discovered my true passion. For the first time I had found my true path.

Influence Tool 49
Know that everything happens for a reason

Before this discovery, I had thought my true path was trading. Now don't get me wrong, I loved it.

I would stay up all night reading trading books, spend all evening analysing the markets and all day shouting across the trading floor to sales traders, making a market in UK equities.

But something made me step into the CEO's office after a couple of years on the trading floor and try to become a corporate financier.

After several lunches, three rejections and nine meetings, I got my offer in corporate finance.

On my first week in the new role I knew it was not for me, but I was not one to quit and I made myself find what I loved about the role.

What I did love was the meetings with the business founders, the meetings with the VCs and the meetings with the VC fund managers as they told me their stories of how they created something from just the belief that they could do it.

When listening to these people, I was truly in the zone and for the very first time I knew that 100%, without a doubt in my mind, business, private equity and venture capital was my thing, my true calling, my passion, my life, my unique contribution.

After a meeting with one of my colleagues in corporate finance, Patrick, who worked on preparing companies for initial public offerings, he took me with him to meet a venture capital fund manager to determine if we could take some of his investments into the pre-IPO stage.

Influence Tool 50
More harm is done by indecision than wrong decision

After that meeting a decision was made in my mind.

At all these meetings I would find myself asking questions about the founder, the creator, how they took this bundle of risk and turned it into a reality.

Influence Tool 51
Be quick to make decisions and accept responsibility when they go wrong

---

My decision was made. I wanted to learn how to create a business out of nothing and one day I too wanted to work with private businesses through private equity.

So from this moment on, my goal was to set up in business, learn the ropes and build a portfolio of private equity investments.

Once the decision was made, I searched for all the evidence in my past to back up the belief that I was born for business.

Memories of my first car washing business at age 12 where I was earning an average of £16 a day came back to me; the first magazine I published for wrestling fans at age 14; my first advertising contract I sealed for free at age 16 promoting my wrestling video business; the times I got my Dad to drive me to car boot sales first thing on a Sunday morning to find bargain wrestling memorabilia so I could trade them in for a mark-up outside the Coulston Hall in Bristol.

I eventually ceased trading in my wrestling business when I moved to London to commence my studies at Kingston University.

I didn't have the grades to get into a top university as, rather than studying hard for my A-levels, I was more interested in running a business.

As I searched my memory database for evidence to back up the belief, I came to a huge realisation.

Influence Tool 52
*Look for clues in your childhood
to find your passion*

I started university with over £10,000 in the bank, all self-created, and for some reason over a three-year period I lost the entrepreneurial spirit I had before university, and instead of continuing in business I found myself applying for graduate schemes.

After my first 100-odd rejections from banks and financial institutions, rather than finding an entrepreneurial way in or starting up in business again, I found myself returning to university where I got myself into significant debt while undertaking my Masters.

After another year of learning from professors, I found myself going for round two of rejections (that's over 200 now).

I don't know when, I don't know how, I don't know why, but after four years of studying at university all my entrepreneurial spirit had been sucked out of me and all I could think about was my first class degree, my Masters and graduate schemes. But I found that no company was interested in my academic achievements and I became very frustrated.

I had lost my soul and spirit and was doing everything the same way as everyone else. I had become a sheep.

I found myself with a first class degree from a non-recognised university, some poor A-level results, a Masters, all the debt from the tuition fees and a job at Selfridges serving customers in the retail sector that was outside of my dream.

I had an obsession to work in banking and finance, but over 200 rejection letters were piled up in the corner of my flat in Sackville Street, Manchester.

In my Banking and Finance Professional Program, I recount how this led to a feeling of depression and I walk people through the process of taking this feeling and controlling it to produce big results in banking and finance. But to cut this long story short, I developed my methodology of modelling success in this moment of depression.

Eventually, I got a mentor who taught me how to influence my way into banking and finance the unorthodox way and I got my first offer as tea boy in TD Waterhouse, leading to my broking role, market making role in London, corporate finance role and the situation I find myself in today.

Now, did all this happen for a reason?

Was all this part of my destiny?

I am not here to go into beliefs about destiny, but everything in my life when channelled through the brain of a well-trained RAS has developed the belief that this was all part of the plan.

All these moments have come together to lead to my ultimate mission and the reason I am writing this book today, which is to inspire others to find their path in life and climb to the top in banking and finance.

The sequence of events that occurred following the decision that I was going to start my very own trading consultancy company was uncanny in how they came together.

Influence Tool 53
Reflect upon defining moments in your life

Some would say a guiding force, but I believe decisions have to be made as opportunity presents itself and that decision comes from within.

The decision had been made, the belief had been developed and now only action was to follow.

If you have come to realise that corporate finance is your true passion, you will soon find out that the hours can be seriously intense.

So to set up a business at the same time as working in corporate finance required 5am to 2am shifts, running on three hours' sleep and no weekend rest.

My passion kept me awake, my belief kept me going and my results took a long time to come.

I knew nothing about business, but I knew my philosophy.

Find the top 1% of achievers in anything, put yourself in a position of service to them, find out what they do differently and model the way they do things (and I don't mean plagiarise).

So I set about finding my mentors and role models. I read hundreds of books from Tony Robbins, to Dr Stephen R Covey, to Sun Zu - The Art of War, from Richard Branson to Steve Jobs to Peter Hargreaves to Warren Buffet and everything in between.

Influence Tool 54
Invest in the books and training of the people you want to connect with

I attended countless seminars from business leaders; I spent every penny I earned on educating myself from the 1% who had achieved results in every aspect of business.

After a few months of modelling the best and taking action, I realised that I had no money left, even though I was on an above average salary and bonus.

So to fund my business and training, I took out credit cards; I was hungry to learn and build contacts, and the fastest way to get access to the people I wanted to connect with was to pay for their training.

The debt actually built and built and built and I found myself in the ridiculous position of schmoozing clients in the day as an investment banker, networking with entrepreneurs in the evening, implementing during lunch breaks and weekends and bizarrely beyond broke.

Everybody around me thought that I was coining it in with my investment banking role.

In fact, it got so bad that one morning on my way to work I had maxed out all credit cards.

I had already spent my wages on getting my website designed, the company incorporated and legal fees for terms and conditions and the countless other expenses which seemed to come up when getting started with my trading consultancy company.

I actually found myself in a situation where I could not afford to get on the tube and I was late for work.

There was no point turning back to the house to get more money as there was none. So in a moment of decision, I let my ethics slip and jumped the barrier to the train when no one was looking.

It was so early in the morning that there were very few people at Fulham Broadway station.

I scampered onto the District line tube, took out my Richard Branson biography and buried my head in shame behind the book. Ironically, the chapter I was reading recounted Richard Branson's night in prison after evading tax on his imports of records from France.

He recounts how this was the best thing that ever happened to him as it set him on the straight and narrow early on.

A couple of train changes later, I reached Waterloo station.

I got off the Northern line to change for the Waterloo and City line to Bank station.

Suddenly, two security guards pulled me aside and asked me for my ticket.

I panicked and had to come clean. After taking all my details, they escorted me out of the station and I ran to Old Broad Street, late for work.

A week later, a letter came through the door asking if I pleaded guilty or not guilty. I raised my hand and pleaded guilty.

Another week later, a fine for £100 came through the door that I could not afford to pay.

I needed to buy a laptop and I had already committed, so I procrastinated and kept putting the letter on the bottom of the pile of things to do.

Two weeks later, I arrived at my desk at KBC and I was asked to come into the office to speak with the HR Manager, Jane.

Jane had received a letter demanding that they take the £100 fine from my wages and she wanted to know what the fine was for.

I put my hands up in shame and in embarrassment explained that I had no money and jumped the gate at Fulham Broadway station.

Jane could not understand why I could not afford a £100 fine with the money they were paying me.

I had no way of explaining and made up a story about how I was late and forgot my wallet. I left the meeting room and returned to my desk.

They had to take it seriously as there are very strict guidelines about FSA approval and approved persons in investment banks.

I had hit a decisive point in my life. Have you ever hit a point in your life where you have to make a decision that could alter your path forever? Well this was one of them for me.

Influence Tool 55
Face tough decisions head on

Not to get all heebie-jeebie on you, but this was the sign I was looking for.

After the meeting was over, I returned to my desk and made a decision.

I had to follow my passion and have belief in my ability.

I was getting nowhere juggling my corporate finance job and setting up my trading consultancy.

I was in debt and needed to start closing contracts in my business.

I returned to Jane's office five minutes later and caught her just as she was leaving.

I told Jane the whole truth, and nothing but the truth. I explained that business was my passion and I had been setting up a trading consultancy and that I wanted to hand in my notice.

After a lot of questions, Jane wished me the best and asked me one final time, "Are you sure you want to do this?" to which I responded "yes" with certainty and walked out immediately without notice.

As I held price-sensitive insider information, there was no notice period and my bags were checked for price-sensitive information as I walked out anxiously to begin a new chapter in my life.

I did not know where the next penny was coming from, but I walked down the street smugly as I knew I had made the right decision.

Influence Tool 56
Put yourself in a position where you have to make it happen

Now I had to find a way, or make a way. There was no third option.

By completely stepping outside of my comfort zone, I had created an environment where my dream had to become a reality, I was following my passion.

The road ahead was hard and bumpy, but one by one I slowed down and drove over every speed bump until I hit the motorway where a whole new set of problems began, but I had built the emotional muscle to handle anything that was thrown at me.

In my first month I sealed £30,000 of new business; in my second month I started trading for additional income and presenting my trading ideas at seminars for private investors for the first time ever; in my first year we sealed contracts with Man Group, ODL, TD Waterhouse, Bloomberg and City Index.

In my second year I had Peter Hargreaves as my business angel, with an office in the City of London and multiple staff.

In my third year I was invited to over 200 universities to coach students and graduates on earning more, achieving more and getting more offers in banking and finance.

Five years on and I own three businesses in banking and finance and I am truly living my dream.

I now have the resources to follow my mission of creating a bank for the people under a system that works.

Influence Tool 57
Define your mission and say it every day

Through Metal Monkey Private Equity I get to help businesses adjust to the changing markets and turn businesses around by utilising technology to strip out much of the overhead.

Through my Banking and Finance Professional Programs, I get to work with the next generation of banking and finance leaders, helping students and graduates to overcome the problems faced with earning more, achieving more and getting more offers in banking and finance. I also get a constant flow of talent for my new banking venture.

Through my Professional Trader Programs and trading consultancy I get to stay in touch with my passion for the financial markets.

Through my mission to reform money I get to work on a mission that will have a huge impact on poverty, peace and economic stability.

It has all come together like clockwork.

Influence Tool 58
Ask yourself questions that inspire action

▼ What defining moments have happened in your life?

▼ What seemingly small decisions have you made that have changed your destiny?

▼ What beliefs do you have right now that hold you back from taking the action you need to take?

▼ What beliefs would you need in order to achieve your big, fat, hairy goal?

▼ What can you do right now to empower yourself with the beliefs you need to set the spiral in motion?

▼ What will happen if you don't believe you can climb to the top?

▼ What will your life look like in five years time if you don't develop the belief that allows you to take the action you know you should be taking?

▼ What about ten years from now?

▼ What would your life look like in five years time if you started to take action right now?

▼ What has happened in your life that seemed traumatic at the time, but has led you to this moment right now where you are reading this book?

▼ What are you going to do about it?

▼ Are you going to be a 'wet blanket' or a 'happiness thief'?

▼ Are you going to be a 'dry toast'?

▼ Are you going to be a sceptic like 99%, or are you willing to believe that your big, fat, hairy goal could become a reality like it does for the 1%?

Well, once you know what you want, you are willing to do it and you believe you can do it, you will need to dare to be different...

CHAPTER SIX

Dare To Be Different

influence your way to the top in banking and finance

"I think if you look at people who haven't had any moral compass, who've just changed to say whatever they thought the popular thing was, in the end they're losers."

Michael Bloomberg

Influence Tool 59
Don't follow the crowd

At the time of writing, Michael Bloomberg is the 10th richest person in the United States, having a net worth of US$18 billion in 2010. Michael Bloomberg has prided himself on his ability to stand by what he believes in and, without a doubt, he dared to be different.

▼ What makes a Michael Bloomberg different?

▼ What makes a John D Rockefeller?

▼ A JP Morgan?

▼ A Warren Buffett?

▼ A Charles Schwab?

Names that will live in financial history for ever.

In this chapter I would like to get into specific strategy. In giving you a formula to get your foot in the door, I would also like to share my observation on what makes these financial legends different.

In a nutshell, they dared to be different.

In an interview, Michael Bloomberg once responded, "I have an ego that tells me anything is possible if you work hard."

After a successful career at Salomon Brothers (now owned by Citigroup), where he had become a general partner, heading up equity trading and, later, systems development, he was fired from Salomon Brothers during its takeover.

What might have been a negative experience for some turned out to be the making of the Michael Bloomberg we know today and the reason we all trade from a screen with his name on it.

Just as JP Morgan who 'always tried to turn every disaster into an opportunity', Bloomberg went on to set up Innovative Market Systems.

Merrill Lynch became their first customer and went on to invest $30 million in Bloomberg's vision. The company was renamed Bloomberg LP in 1986.

By 1987, it had installed 5,000 of its computer terminals in financial institutions.

As of 2009, the company had more than 250,000 terminals worldwide.

Influence Tool 60
Give at least 10% of everything you make to a charity you believe in

---

As I write, Bloomberg works for $1 a year as Mayor of New York and donates to causes he believes in through his Bloomberg Family Foundation.

"I am a big believer in giving it all away and have always said that the best financial planning ends with bouncing the check to the undertaker."

One thing is for certain, Bloomberg dared to be different and still does to this day.

Influence Tool 61
Study people who don't achieve their goals and do the opposite

---

The theme of this chapter may be obvious, but it is very rarely acted upon. If 99% of students and graduates will not climb to the top in their area of passion, if 99% will not set a big, fat, hairy goal, let alone achieve it, then all you need to do is find out what they do and do the opposite.

In fact, Warren Buffett (currently ranked the 3rd wealthiest man in the world) frequently attributes his financial success to doing the opposite of everybody else.

"We simply attempt to be fearful when others are greedy and to be greedy only when others are fearful."Warren Buffett

Daring to be different, alongside modelling success, has been one of the instrumental tools in my life that has allowed me to fulfill my definition of success and one of the main principles that has helped students and graduates with whom I have worked to get countless offers and opportunities at almost every major financial institution worldwide.

This book was never written as a step by step application, CV or interview advice book (I have training programs to fill in all those gaps), but rather to provide the motivation to let you know what you can achieve when you put your mind to it, and give you some of the tools that you can use in your journey to climbing to the top in banking and finance.

Influence Tool 62
Your approach to securing a career is a reflection of your approach in work

---

However, a journey of a thousand steps begins with your first step, in the form of your first offer.

So in demonstrating how important it is to be different in climbing to the top in banking and finance, I think it is worth dedicating a chapter to some of the key aspects through which I coach students and graduates in climbing to the top and getting their first foot in the door.

Charles Schwab, the legend who helped negotiate the secret sale of Carnegie Steel to a group of financiers led by JP Morgan summed it up best:"All successful employers are stalking men who will do the unusual, men who think, men who attract attention by performing more than is expected of them."

It goes without saying that, in our time, the same applies to women who aspire to climb to the top too.

Doing things differently from everyone else takes risk, guts and belief.

It begins from the moment you meet a contact, the moment you construct your CV, the moment you type your first application; in fact this is the time when you need to show how different you are the most.

Not by talking, but by demonstrating how different your approach to securing a career is to everybody else's.

Influence Tool 63
If you are waiting for a job to be advertised, you are probably too late

---

Everyone else will follow the same process and that is exactly how they tend to perform for the company – the same as everyone else.

Your strategy for getting your first foot in the door is your greatest opportunity to prove your difference.

In this chapter I am going to walk you through a 10-step framework with some of the key distinctions that will make you different in getting your first foot in the door for your ideal role in banking and finance.

Influence Tool 64
The order in which you do things can significantly change your results

---

Syntax is often defined as a systematic, orderly arrangement.

I refer to syntax for the purpose of this chapter as the order and sequence in which activities are undertaken.

From the Ancient Greek word for 'arrangement', it literally means the study of the principles and rules for constructing sentences in natural language.

In my teaching and coaching, syntax is a defining factor in climbing to the top in banking and finance.

Take, for example, the general approach of securing your ideal role in banking and finance.

Here are the general steps most will advise you on in securing a career in banking and finance, and the path that 99% will follow:

Step 1 - *Get good grades and go to a Top 10 university*

Step 2 - *Construct your CV*

Step 3 - *Apply for graduate schemes*

Step 4 - *Attend interviews and assessment centres*

Step 5 - *If no joy, add your CV to job boards*

Step 6 - *Enroll with recruitment companies*

Step 7 - *If no joy, get realistic and try something else*

Here is a 1% approach:

Step 1 - *Decide what you want*

Step 2 - *Identify the top 1% in your industry to model*

Step 3 - *Become a Key Person of Influence within your niche*

Step 4 - *Innovate your value propositions*

Step 5 - *Construct your evidence document*

Step 6 - *Make contact with the top 1%*

Step 7 - *Deliver a series of value propositions*

Step 8 - *Close your contacts into opportunities*

Step 9 - *Close the interview the way business people do it*

Step 10 - *Keep delivering value and change your approach until you are in*

The order and sequence of events is extremely important.

99% will be meeting their potential employer for the first time during interview. Doing it the 1% way, this will be the final step in closing all the good work and relationship building that you have already done so far.

Now, I am not saying that you will never secure a job the 99% way; I am saying that most people won't, and if you secure your job the 99% way, I know from interviewing, working alongside and meeting the top 1% that very few at the top started the 99% way.

So all in all, if you are following what the careers experts, books, universities, careers advisors and 99% are telling you, the likelihood of you climbing to the top in banking and finance is statistically very slim.

If you listen to conventional advice, climbing to the top is reserved for a handful of top university elites.

I would like to start you on your journey to knowing what you really need to do to climb to the top and secure your offer the 1% way.

It will mean that you need to decide if you are going to do it; it will mean that you need to be willing to do it; it will mean that you need to believe you can do it; and it will mean that you have agreed to dare to be different from what everybody else is doing.

It does not require you to be one of the handful of elite who got the top grades from the top universities.

It is different from what everybody else who has not climbed to the top will tell you, and it will probably be offensive to conventional careers advisors, but it is what works now, what worked in the past and what will work in any economy in the future, recession or no recession.

If you would like more clarity on how everybody else is doing it the 99% way, then just Google free information on the internet, buy some careers books, attend company presentations and get conventional careers advice, as it is readily available everywhere.

Step 1 - Decide what you want

"Singleness of purpose is one of the chief essentials for success in life, no matter what may be one's aim."

John D Rockefeller

When a student or graduate enrolls on my Banking and Finance Professional Program, we give them a Chartered Institute for Securities and Investments (CISI) endorsed and accredited crash course in banking and finance, psychometrically assess them and consult them to make sure they know which of the ten main sectors in banking and finance they are going for.

> ## Influence Tool 65
> *Spend a lot of time getting clear about what you want, it will save you years of heartache*

If John D Rockefeller, who became the world's richest man and the first American worth more than a billion dollars (adjusting for inflation, he is often regarded as the richest person in history) has been quoted as saying 'singleness of purpose' is the key to success, then deciding what we want has to be our first step.

In a previous chapter and knowledge bite I broke banking and finance up into ten main sectors.

> ## Influence Tool 66
> *If you are applying for more than one sector, in most cases you probably have an average application, interview and CV*

The importance of focus has already been hammered into you throughout this book, but for each sector in banking and finance you will be pursuing different goals, you will spend your time differently, you will be meeting different people, you will be applying differently, you will have a different CV, the language you use will be different, your entry strategy will be different, your time at university will be spent differently and the companies you apply to will be different depending on which of the ten main sectors is in line with your passion, your big, fat, hairy banking and finance goal and how fast you want to climb to the top.

Once you are clear, you are ready to identify your models...

Step 2 - Identify the top 1% in your industry and model

> ## Influence Tool 67
> *Spend most of your time with people who are one thousand steps ahead of your current game*

"It's better to hang out with people better than you. Pick out associates whose behavior is better than yours and you'll drift in that direction."

Warren Buffett

As the teacher, mentor and philosophical source for Warren Buffett, Benjamin Graham pioneered the way for the modern era's single most successful investor. His contribution and legacy are unmatched by any other single investor of the 20th century.

From a very early age, Warren Buffett knew that the path to success was to find your role models, read their books, research their stories, find out their path, find out everything you can about them, then get yourself in a position where you can work with them as Warren Buffett did with legendary investor Benjamin Graham.

Focus all your efforts in finding out what is required to work in your sector from the top, find out how your role models did it and proceed with the intention of one day working alongside them.

JP Morgan understood this when he advised,

"When you expect things to happen - strangely enough - they do happen."

What qualification would they want you to have? What training would they want you to complete before you meet them? What skills really led to their success? What is their definition of value? What value can you add to their lives?

Find out everything.

Warren Buffett knew how he could help Benjamin Graham when he got his first foot in the door.

Aged 22, Buffett discovered Benjamin Graham was on the board of GEICO Insurance.

Taking a train to Washington DC on a Saturday, he knocked on the door of GEICO's headquarters until a janitor allowed him in. There he met Lorimer Davidson, GEICO's Vice President, and the two discussed the insurance business for hours.

Davidson would eventually become Buffett's life-long friend and a lasting influence and later recall that he found Buffett to be an 'extraordinary man' after only fifteen minutes.

Buffett offered to work for Graham for free, but Graham refused.

Influence Tool 68
Invest in training on influence

Buffett returned to Omaha and worked as a stockbroker while taking a Dale Carnegie public speaking course to improve his ability to influence (the subject of the next chapter).

Using what he learned, he felt confident enough to teach 'Investment Principles' and two years later Buffett accepted a job at Benjamin Graham's partnership.

Buffet knew exactly and specifically what he wanted and who he wanted to learn from and continued to deliver value until he got it.

Influence Tool 69
Don't create enemies out of your original mentors

A quick word of caution here: 'modelling' and 'copying' are very different.

You want to get inside their head and have the intention (even if it never happens) of working alongside them eventually in a mentor and disciple partnership.

I have had many people misinterpret 'modelling' and end up making a rival out of their mentor by creating a rival service or copying their business and stories.

For example, over the years I have had students and graduates try and compete with one of my businesses and copy everything we do instead of thinking longer term and modelling the mindset, which involves collaboration rather than competition.

When I wanted to work with Mike Harris, I offered to help him in areas where I knew I could add value and proceeded to structure a collaborative joint venture partnership, rather than competing.

This is a business analogy, I know, but still applies in your career.

Influence Tool 70
Guard your reputation and try to make as few enemies as possible

---

You only get one chance at your reputation in banking and finance; your name can take years to build and seconds to be destroyed.

You want to operate out of the highest integrity at all times.

Heed the words of Warren Buffett:

"It takes 20 years to build a reputation and five minutes to ruin it. If you think about that, you'll do things differently."

Once you have identified your models, you are ready to become a Key Person of Influence (KPI)...

Step 3 - Become a Key Person of Influence (KPI) within your niche

> ### Influence Tool 71
> *In every sector in banking and finance there are key people of influence with whom you want to develop a strategy to connect*

I first heard the phrase 'Key Person of Influence' from a very good friend of mine and author of the book Become A Key Person of Influence (KPI), Daniel Priestley.

You can listen to an interview I did with Daniel Priestley on becoming a key person of influence in banking and finance by visiting **www.climbing-to-the-top.com**

Having worked alongside Daniel Priestley, Mike Harris and other KPIs to coach entrepreneurs who want to build their brands as a key person within their industry, I have had an exclusive insider's look into what the make-up and workings are behind key people of influence within multiple sectors.

Michael Bloomberg, Mike Harris, Peter Hargreaves, JP Morgan, Warren Buffett and the countless others mentioned in this book all meet the KPI criteria.

While the KPI formula of becoming a published author, product creator, pitch genius and web famous expert who gets multiple joint venture offers in a targeted niche sector of an industry applies to expert business owners, the application of the KPI principles for students and graduates seeking careers in banking and finance is unquestionable.

Your goal is to become a key person in your chosen field of passion within banking and finance, which is easier than you may think.

In his book, Daniel puts people into three main categories: newbies, worker bees and KPIs.

Newbies work hard in the short term in the belief that the rewards will come later; they have seen the rewards that somebody in the inner circle has achieved and would like to create similar results for themselves.

They are full of energy and enthusiasm and are willing to go the extra mile to reach the inner circle.

Influence Tool 72
Don't become a 'worker bee'

The worker bees, on the other hand, have been doing the work for a while now and are not really getting anywhere; they have had some of the dream knocked out of them as they feel they have not received the success they deserve relative to the work they have put in.

They start to blame forces outside of themselves for their lack of success and start to feel resentment to the KPIs and the enthusiasm of the newbies.

They become sceptical and move into new challenges frequently.

Each time they move and switch, their focus and efforts move into a new niche sector (or application in your case).

This means they have to start building momentum and knowledge over and over again.

They drift from opportunity to opportunity, never really receiving the rewards that originally motivated them and inspired them to work so hard.

They start to settle and watch their big, fat, hairy goals drift away.

In the inner circle of the industry there are key people of influence who make everything look easy.

They live in the inner circle, so they are always having opportunities fly around for them. They have emails sent to them every day with new opportunities and they sort for the best ones.

They are so connected that within a few phone calls they can put people together and make magic happen.

All their deals are done over lunch and dinner meetings in fancy restaurants or on boats and planes.

A new student or graduate will normally start as a newbie (as I did) and go to university with all the enthusiasm of one day becoming an investment banker, for example, having met a rich investment banker in the past, watched a film, read a book or gained some work experience in the industry and being inspired and attracted to the lifestyle, wealth, image, status or whatever it is for you.

After graduating from university, having followed all the traditional careers advice, most get rejected, work harder, but never really make the progress they desire.

Influence Tool 73
Never cling on to excuses, accept responsibility for everything

---

Eventually they get fed up of the rejection and begin to blame forces around them for their lack of success.

It's the recession, or it's because I am an international student, or it's because I didn't go to the top university, or the most common excuse: it's because I don't have the experience.

A side point, but a question I ask of all who try to use lack of experience as their excuse:

"Is anybody in the world born with experience?"

Or has every single person who works in banking and finance had to figure out how to overcome that hurdle?

You know the answer, how you overcome this hurdle is a reflection of how creative you may be in the role.

Worker bees eventually start to resent the KPIs and cling on to an excuse as they endlessly apply for opportunity after opportunity.

Every time they choose a new sector or new path they have to start again and never build any momentum in any sector of banking and finance.

Eventually they settle for just an average job that does not fulfill them or make them happy.

They end up seeing work as a necessity and cannot wait for Friday night in order to forget about the week just gone.

As Friday night approaches they experience an all-week high, but start to feel a sense of depression as the weekend ends and Monday looms just around the corner.

You see them on the tube or subway every morning, miserable as they travel in for another day at work, counting the time until lunch and celebrating at the end of the day.

When I work with students and graduates, my goal is to carve a strategy to make sure they achieve KPI status.

Influence Tool 74
The more connected you are, the more valuable you become

The rules are simple: the most connected wins and the connections come from delivering results in advance and offering value consistently, not just every now and then.

Becoming a KPI has nothing to do with academic achievement and can be achieved by anyone from any background, with a bit of conscious effort and clever strategy.

You will need to dare to be different and work through this 10-step formula.

At first it may seem tricky as it may not be what you are used to; as time goes on, it becomes second nature and part of your subconscious.

When you are a KPI, finding new opportunity is never an effort.

In fact, a little study of the biggest brand name business people and KPIs in the industry and you will find out that the majority do not come from a high academic background at all, in fact quite the opposite.

Influence Tool 75
Develop a strategy to become connected from your first year at university so you don't need to apply upon graduation

They knew the inner circle secrets and started building their KPI status early while everybody else was busy studying and trying to get their foot in the door at graduate schemes.

Once you have developed your KPI plan, you are ready to innovate your Value Propositions (VP)...

Step 4 - Innovate your Value Propositions (VP)

> ## Influence Tool 76
> ### *The more you give, the more you get*

"Think of giving not as a duty but as a privilege.

"John D Rockefeller Jr.

One of the main reasons people do not climb to the top is because they never develop that invaluable art of value creation.

Once they become aware and make a conscious effort to become connected in their sector of speciality in banking and finance, they go on a mission to meet as many people in their industry as they can.

They tune their RAS to see opportunity that they were blind to before.

Most students and graduates when faced with the opportunity to meet a new influential connection, let's say at a university company presentation, see this as their big opportunity to try and get some information out of the contact or try and get an immediate favour.

> ## Influence Tool 77
> ### *Think bigger than asking influential people for favours*

While there is value in the information they will give you and you may just get that favour over those who don't ask, there is a lot more you are missing out on.

Rather than using this one-off rare opportunity to get information or get a favour, 1% people have a much bigger plan.

They are more strategic and seek ways of becoming their friends and delivering genuine value to the contact. Later, they may ask for information or a favour once they have done plenty for them first and delivered lots of value.

Influence Tool 78
Don't ask for sex in the first five minutes

The way most people approach contacts is like meeting somebody for the first time and asking for their hand in marriage or inviting them back to their place to stay over after three minutes of conversation.

Now in some cultures this is normal, but in other cultures there is normally a gradual courting process.

You see somebody that you like, you try to catch their eye and attention and test the water, you approach them, you find out about them and then you ask them for a small commitment like a telephone number after demonstrating why you are not like the others or a waste of time.

In order to do this you ask questions, you find out about their interests and you align yourself with what they are interested in.

If you are smart, you offer them help and value in something that they are trying to achieve.

You then call them, speak with them and take the commitment one step further as you get an agreement for you to take them out for dinner.

Influence Tool 79
Take small steps with your contacts

If you have not done the work before this well, and go straight for the dinner proposal, most of the time you get declined.

You have to earn the date and gradually you make progress towards asking for their hand in marriage or, depending on your goal, an invitation back to your place.

While asking enough people if they will marry you or sleep with you within five minutes of meeting them may work if you do it enough times, most would agree the courting option is a lot more effective and likely to lead to the result and a sustainable long-term partnership.

Even in slightly different cultures and arranged marriages, the parents do the courting process on behalf of their child.

There is a best practice and process that leads to the desired result more effectively than closing a new contact in the first few minutes of meeting them, like most do when meeting KPIs.

This is because a meeting with a KPI is a rare opportunity for them as they have not built the KPI status yet, and we have to all start somewhere.

Influence Tool 80
See the world as your team

I started with my mentor in Leeds and grew my contacts consciously and strategically by delivering more value than anybody else was willing to give consistently.

The irony is that once you reach KPI status you can fast-track the whole process as they either know you already or have been introduced to you by somebody they respect and trust and you have the ability to cut straight to the close, but I still prefer to offer value first, no matter what.

Influence Tool 81
You want to become a value creator, rather than a value extractor

Most people try and extract as much value out of their contacts as they can because they believe that this is their one big chance.

I have a rule in business: I will never ask for anything unless I can deliver ten times more value than I want in return up front.

Whenever I target a contact that I would like to do business with, I sit down and innovate the value that I can give to them so that they respond to me amongst all the noise that most busy people have to filter through.

You will be amazed at how effective and simple this will be if you train your RAS to continually focus on giving value to others before asking for anything in return.

In fact, I have a Facebook group just for students and graduates seeking careers in banking and finance that shares contacts and helps each other develop VP as their career progresses in banking and finance.

It is called 'Banking Careers By Benedix' and I suggest you join the community.

In fact, as I write I just noticed the following message posted on the wall:

It really works!

I applied Simon's value offering skills at a meeting with a Director of a boutique and sent him a thank you letter as soon as I went home after the meeting. I received his reply mail this morning, and here it is:

Hi Shengyong, I would like to schedule another meeting with you whenever you are free so that we can consider some business development opportunities. I have a lot of time availability Wednesday to Friday, so let me know a suitable day / time for you.

They are on their way to KPI status as I write.

The world of delivering value is one full of prosperity, abundant opportunity and a whole lot more fun than trying to extract value out of everybody that you meet.

There is less rejection, you do not feel pushy and the results grow exponentially.

Train your RAS to think in terms of value and watch the offers flood in.

Cialdini in his book *Influence* discusses the power of what he calls the Law of Reciprocity.

The law states that if you give to people what you would like in return, people feel compelled to comply and return the favour.

Use it with ethics and good intention and your success to the top is guaranteed.

Once you are clear about your VP, you are ready to construct your Evidence Document, (ED)...

Step 5 - Construct your Evidence Document (ED)

> ### Influence Tool 82
> *Always discuss actual, quantifiable results rather than loose statements*

I don't like the words 'CV' or 'resumé' because so many people use them incorrectly.

99% use a CV to list everything they have done in the past that they are proud of. In fact, even if you write a really good CV or resumé using expert advice or one of the many books on the topic, I still think most will have a 99% CV.

The reason is that a CV or resumé done the 1% way can only be written once you know what niche sector in banking and finance you are going for, and most will teach you how to write a generic CV.

I like to call a 1% CV a tailored Evidence Document (ED).

If you are writing a CV or resumé without focus on the type of company and sector you are applying for, it is one that will go in the shredder with the rest of them.

An ED is results based, specific for the results the department wishes to receive and uses some very influential ninja tricks in order to get a lot of information on no more than one page.

You need to be armed and ready with this as KPIs never know when they will need it as the opportunity floods in.

If you would like to download a sample (sample for modelling only...don't plagiarise) that I wrote for one of my clients which got three offers at an investment bank, trading house and hedge fund when pursuing a career in trading, then visit www.WhichFinanceJob.com and you can download it as my gift for reading this far.

I get emails all the time from students who are swamped with phone calls for interviews the minute they change their CV to an ED.

Try it and you will see.

Influence Tool 83
Do not wait for somebody to request your ED for you to write it

---

You want to impress by having your ED ready within five minutes after a request.

You will come across as someone who is ready for opportunity. It is one of your essential tools that you have ready to give to your contacts after you have delivered value.

Not upon first contact like most (unless requested of course), and certainly not asking your contacts to check if your CV is OK as most do during company presentations.

The ED comes into play once you have delivered value and you ask for a return favour of a friend, in the form of career opportunities.

The syntax is very important.

Value first, and lots of it, then opportunity will come your way and the ED is included as part of your proposition once you have reached that stage in the partnership.

Once you have your ED, you are ready to make contact...

Step 6 - Make contact with the 1%

Once you have your VP lined up and your ED is ready, you are ready to start building your KPI status and connecting with the other KPIs in your niche sector.

There are several ways of making contact that I teach; emailed propositions are the most common and, at the same time, the least effective.

Influence Tool 84
Find out where the KPIs in your sector hang out

By far the most effective is by being one of their customers where they have to speak to you and then delivering a VP at a seminar, over the phone or in person.

It requires that you part with some money, though, in order to move forward.

An ideal VP will be different for each sector and is beyond the scope of this book.

For some free videos on how to move forward with this, visit **www.BankingAndFinanceProgram.com** and you will be sent a free video series and many more resources to help you on your journey.

Remember, the key to making contact, as always, is simply to do the opposite of everybody else. Here is what most people do when they make contact.

Firstly, as discussed already, most will approach contacts by asking for something and extracting value, so the first thing is simply to contact people with suggestions of how you can help them and add value.

Secondly, everybody else will be sending CVs blindly with a cover email pitching their education.

99% of emails from students and graduates begin with something like 'Hi, my name is....and I am an MBA from....'

Introducing yourself as your education is the worst introduction you can give.

Most busy contacts know that they are going to be asking for something and normally hit the delete key at this point.

Your emails will get read if you discuss what is important to them and hook them in.

I have a whole program dedicated to making written contact with KPIs that templates every step in constructing a VP and converting contacts into offers.

As a start though, you should claim your free videos at **www.BankingAndFinanceProgram.com**

Thirdly, everybody else will be writing long emails; quite simply, busy people do not have time to read long emails about your education.

Think of what emails you read and delete. You read the ones from friends or colleagues, ones that you have consented to receive, and the ones that offer value in topics that you are interested in, right?

If a stranger emails you with a generic email that is clearly written for lots of people pitching things that don't matter to you, you delete it, right?

This approach wastes your time, their time and is highly ineffective. It is the path of 99% of job seekers who are applying outside of the graduate schemes.

Remember, time is your greatest asset. So stop doing what everybody else is doing, do the opposite and channel your energy into what works.

Once you have made contact, you are ready to deliver value...

Step 7 - Deliver a series of VPs

When I work with students and graduates, I actually give them a points system to know when they are ready to close their contacts for work opportunities.

There are different types of VPs that lead to different points with KPIs, but you are only ready to ask in return once you have reached the stage of business friendship.

As John D Rockefeller put it: 'A friendship founded on business is better than a business founded on friendship'. When I want to strike a new business partnership, as mentioned before, I deliver multiple VPs – not just the one but on multiple occasions – and opportunity comes back in abundance.

I have repeated this point here because repetition is the mother of all achievement.

Train your RAS to give value and your journey to the top will be easier than you can imagine.

Once you have delivered enough value, you are ready to close...

Step 8 - Close your contacts into opportunities

There comes a time when you need to capitalise on all your hard work and close contacts into opportunities.

Influence Tool 85
Request from others in a way that is focused on them

The topic of the next chapter is the number one skill in your journey to the top – influence and your ability to communicate with people.

No matter where you are, what you have done or how much value you have added, if you cannot influence and inspire people into your vision, then nothing will happen.

Learning how to close contacts into interviews and opportunities will be the greatest skill you ever invest in.

Not only is it the skill that gets you the job and allows you to climb to the top, but it is the same skill that makes you the most valuable in the institution.

"The ability to deal with people is as purchasable a commodity as sugar or coffee and I will pay more for that ability than for any other under the sun."

John D Rockefeller

If you have delivered value up to this point, it will be an easy task once you add a few influence skills to the mix.

But nothing will drive forward your ability to climb to the top faster than learning the skills of the top 1% of influencers in the world.

Think about this.

If you have been in a debate, been in a relationship, done anything that involved other people, you would have used some influencing skills.

If you were not influencing, then you were being influenced. Nothing moves unless it is influenced by somebody.

Learning how to influence is the skill of all skills and is the topic of the next chapter.

Influence Tool 86
Think win/win/win or no deal at all

One closing tip on this point: it is very important to have the right intentions.

If you have followed along up to this point, you have delivered value and you are acting in integrity, applying for the role you are passionate about and can add most value, the influencing techniques will work like magic.

That is why it is important to be going for roles that are in line with your passion where you can offer genuine value.

To close your contacts at this point, you must have sufficient levels of reciprocity.

Now you deliver a no-brainer pitch offering more of what you have already done for them when you work together and assume the close with conviction, congruency and confidence, before they offer you Step 9.

Step 9 - Close the interview the way business people do it!

Notice how closing the interview is Step 9.

Most people meet their contacts for the first time at interview.

KPIs have informal interviews over lunch, just to seal the deal on the value that they can add and discuss the details and hurdles that must be overcome to seal the deal.

1% applicants and KPIs are invited to interview in the same manner.

The interview is the final encounter before the contract and handshake is made.

Influence Tool 87
Know the names of all the KPIs in your department before meeting for interview

---

Now, if you are doing interviews the 99% way, your job is harder as you will be meeting for the first time, so I have all my students and graduates build contacts within the company prior to the interview with some clever strategic moves where they get a list of contacts by doing a quick survey within the department for which they are interviewing. But there are several important techniques of influence that can be used to pass all interviews which will be discussed in the next chapter.

Once you have been interviewed, you are ready to move the relationship forward...

Step 10 - Keep delivering value and change your approach until you are in

"I do not think that there is any other quality so essential to success of any kind as the quality of perseverance. It overcomes almost everything, even nature."

John D Rockefeller

In business to business sales, when I worked in investment banking we would expect a minimum of twelve points of contact or rejection before a business deal would ever move forward when pitching for new business.

It is remarkable how much opportunity is lost simply because people accept the first 'no' and move on in disappointment.

Influence Tool 88
Change your approach until it works

This is your test: how do you handle rejection?

Do you give up or do you try something else?

Just imagine you had the cure for cancer and you needed funding in order to market the cure to all those who needed it the most on their death-beds, including your close family members.

If the first person you spoke to about your cure said 'no', would you give up and move on?

If you could save millions of people's lives and your family's, what would you do if somebody told you they would not back your cure?

I hope you would not give up, and you would keep going until you found a backer.

I am hoping you would try a new approach each time until you found what worked.

Eventually you would figure it out for the good of the world and your family, right?

Well, what if you adopted the same approach with your big, fat, hairy goal?

Your success is guaranteed.

I cannot tell you how many students and graduates I have come across who have been rejected from a graduate scheme, tried a different approach, contacted them again and got the offer purely because they demonstrated their determination and drive.

This is what they are looking for; remember what Charles Schwab said: "You must demonstrate your difference, that is what every employer is looking for."

What makes you different?

You don't give up when everybody else does.

That is the difference between the 1% and the rest.

This whole chapter has been about daring to be different.

Try something, recognise what's working and when it's not working, try a new approach and adjust your approach until you figure out what works.

Stay focused to the original goal and you have the holy grail.

That is the secret from the 1% who climb to the top.

That is how I got my offer as a stockbroker, my offer as a market maker, my offer in corporate finance, my business angel Peter Hargreaves and every other business deal I have ever closed in my professional and business career.

Imagine if Muhammad Yunus had given up on his career at the first sign of rejection.

Muhammad, a Bangladeshi banker, economist and Nobel Peace Prize recipient was a professor of economics when he developed the concepts of microcredit and microfinance.

Through Muhammad's determination and ability to refuse to accept 'no' as an answer, loans have been given to entrepreneurs too poor to qualify for traditional bank loans in the most impoverished countries of the world, inspiring a new industry against all odds.

His first attempt at raising finance for the poor ended in rejection. In his own words, "I went to the bank and proposed that they lend money to poor people. The bankers almost fell over."

Did he give up there at the first sign of a 'no'?

After multiple rejections, his next response was simply to make a list of people who needed just a little bit of money.

When the list was complete, there were 42 names and the total amount of money they needed was US$27.

He decided that rejection could not get in the way of what he saw around him.

In his words, "I was teaching in one of the universities while the country was suffering from a severe famine. People were dying of hunger, and I felt very helpless. As an economist, I had no tool in my tool box to fix that kind of situation."

So he decided to get the tools, learn new skills, try new things and get started.

Did he complain that he did not have the tools or the right degree?

No, his first loan, consisting of US$27, was made from his own pocket.

Yunus discovered that a very small loan could make a substantial difference to a poor person so he was not going to stop there.

Yunus believed that, given the chance, the poor will repay the borrowed money and microcredit could be a viable business model, more sustainable than charity – and he was right.

Muhammad Yunus created a vision to eliminate poverty through his own bank.

Before Muhammad Yunus, if you looked at our financial systems around the globe, more than half the population of the world – more than three billion out of six billion people – did not qualify to take out a loan from a bank.

After his initial loan, he wanted to scale and raise more finance. Rejection after rejection came his way, but Yunus finally succeeded in securing a loan from the government Jamata Bank. He changed his approach until he found the right lender.

Yunus's venture continued to operate by securing loans from other banks for its projects.

By 1982, he had 28,000 members. In 1983 the project began operations as a fully-fledged bank and was renamed the Grameen Bank (Village Bank) to make loans to poor Bangladeshis.

But the rejection did not stop there. Yunus and his colleagues encountered everything from violent radicals to political parties who told women that they would be denied a Muslim burial if they borrowed money from the Grameen Bank.

As you climb to the top, your problems do not disappear; they are replaced with bigger hurdles.

Rejection in getting your first foot in the door is the muscle you must develop in climbing to the top.

This is why those who are the most privileged may have a harder time.

Influence Tool 89
Appreciate your misfortunes and learn from them

At least you have experienced the rejection early on and you are developing the muscle that will allow you to climb to the top.

This is what will make you different.

Imagine if you had everything easy, you would not develop this muscle until later in your career.

If you ever get the chance to watch the film *Into The Wild* I recommend it. It recalls the story and experiences of a young man who has everything and his extreme journey to discover himself in the wild.

Contrasting other people's experiences with your own is a great way of realising how privileged we actually are.

Through contrast you can be grateful for any situation as there is always somebody worse off.

The earlier you start realising that climbing to the top is about overcoming rejections, the greater your advantage.

Train your RAS to see the good in everything. The more rejection you get, the stronger you become. Yunus knew this. I learnt this early on.

As of July 2007, Grameen Bank has issued US$6.38 billion to 7.4 million borrowers, having a significant impact on worldwide poverty levels.

The success of the Grameen model of microfinancing has inspired similar efforts in 100 countries throughout the developing world and even in nations like the United States and United Kingdom.

Muhammad has inspired the vision that 'poverty is unnecessary'.

Follow these ten steps and you are following the top 1%; I have seen it time and time again.

▼ Can you afford to give up on your big, fat, hairy goal?

▼ What are the consequences of allowing your fear of rejection to get in the way?

▼ What if Yunus took the first 'no' as his destiny?

▼ What if you spent the next ten years as a worker bee?

▼ Where will you be in five years time if you do not develop the muscle now?

▼ What if you do not commit to mastering the skill of influence?

▼ What if there was one skill that would allow you to earn more, achieve more and get more offers, more than any other?

▼ Would you commit to mastering the skill of influence now, so you can become the KPI and the master of your own destiny?

CHAPTER SEVEN

The Skill Of All Skills To Climb To The Top

influence your way to the top in banking and finance

This whole book has been about giving you tools of influence to climb to the top in banking and finance.

Although it may seem like a lot, there is only really one skill to master, and that is your ability to influence.

When Mike Harris set about transforming banking services, not once, but twice, he was all too aware that everything had boiled down to his ability to influence the CEO of Midland Bank (now HSBC).

But how did a guy who worked in IT get the opportunity to pitch to the CEO?

And how did he walk out with a cheque for £20 million?

Without a shadow of doubt, it was his ability to influence others and influence himself to take massive, bold action where others shy away.

Everyone thought that a bank without branches was a crazy idea, but sure enough the headlines in the newspaper read:

'Home banking comes knocking on the door'

When Midland Bank's chairman, Sir Kit McMahon, described Mike Harris's creation he said, "It represents a radical and exciting new concept which will change the future face of banking. Firstdirect is a breakthrough in which banks deliver services."

But just a few months prior to launch, Mike Harris had no experience in setting up a bank.

Mike Harris influenced his way to pitch to the CEO of Midland Bank for the concept of telephone banking by simply grabbing his attention during the CEO's routine trip around the bank.

When he persuaded his way to his pitch, he had half an hour. Shortly after his meeting, an agreement for a £20 million loan was granted to set up a rival bank to Midland, called Firstdirect.

Before this series of events, Mike Harris had previously worked in the IT department at Midland.

What gave Mike Harris the belief that he could pitch to the CEO?

How did he successfully pitch the concept?

What influenced the CEO to say 'yes'?

Mike Harris, like all the greats mentioned in this book, have truly harnessed the power of influence.

Just as Warren Buffet understood that he needed to brush up on his influencing skills after being rejected for work experience by his mentor Benjamin Graham, you will need to master 'the skill of all skills' to climb to the top in banking and finance.

If ever there were a skill to invest in to climb to the top that will allow you to earn more, achieve more, get more offers and produce an exponential return on investment, this is it.

After his failed attempt to work with his mentor, Warren Buffett went to study under one of the fathers of influence, Dale Carnegie.

After training on the influence skills of public speaking and completing the Carnegie program, Warren Buffett began his journey to becoming the most successful investor of all time.

Buffett understood that to be the best he needed to learn from the best.

He understood that influence is an important part of getting in a position where you can learn from the best, and he set about achieving it.

He did not worry about his lack of qualifications or whether he had an MBA or not, he simply found his way in.

It is interesting to hear what Warren Buffett has to say about MBAs. Search YouTube for his MBA speech. While you are there you can subscribe to my YouTube channel in order to get notified of the latest training videos on The Art Of Offer Attraction in banking and finance by visiting **www.youtube.com/user/studentfinancejobs**

When it did not work out for Buffett, he changed his approach and learnt a thing or two about influence.

We will look into this in more detail in this chapter.

After creating two businesses, both of which had over a billion dollars in annual turnover, Mike Harris went for the hat trick.

He became founding CEO of Prudential Banking's successor, Egg – the first major player in internet banking in the UK and for several years the largest internet bank in the world.

Egg went from start-up, where Mike Harris used his influential pitching skills to secure start-up capital of £80 million, to public in three years when it floated on the London Stock Exchange in July 2000 at a value of £1.3 billion, eventually being sold to Citigroup.

I have had the honour of working alongside Mike Harris as he coaches people on the perfect pitch. In fact, my Platinum Plus

Partners get to learn from Mike Harris first-hand how to construct the perfect pitch for themselves.

I have seen and experienced first-hand what a difference your introduction pitch to contacts can make.

The almighty power of one's ability to influence in climbing to the top in banking and finance is a vital and essential ingredient.

There are some timeless books and principles on influence. This chapter is not meant to compete with some of the core texts of influence like Dale Carnegie's *How To Win Friends And Influence People* or Cialdini's *Influence: The Psychology Of Persuasion*.

It is more of a working example of the principles of influence in action in your banking and finance career.

Graduates of my Banking and Finance Professional Program are invited to join further programs dedicated to the science and art of influence within banking and finance as the subject is really a whole book in itself.

Rather than rework some of the great texts on influence that already exist, this chapter will give you a working strategy of influence in action.

Each step of the strategy will highlight for you some of the key components of influence.

Each step also includes a working example and story of influence in action by banking and finance legends.

This strategy was originally taught to my Platinum Plus Partners after they had met the key people of influence in their industry, had connected successfully, and wanted to deliver VPs to them.

It is a strategy that can be used by you in closing these contacts for work experience and job opportunities, like Warren Buffett did as he started to work alongside his mentor Benjamin Graham.

As your brain adjusts and you consciously programme your RAS to think in terms of value to get your foot in the door, you will need to close your contacts into opportunities.

One part of the strategy involves what I call a 'Six Act Play', which I will introduce you to in this chapter.

'The Six Act Play' is a step by step blueprint for you to follow once you have made contacts and delivered VPs to them.

It is a useful strategy to go through in this chapter as it derives its power from the six main tools of influence that Cialdini identifies in his book Influence.

Act 1 - Deliver your Value Proposition

In the last chapter I discussed the concept of delivering value.

But a deeper discussion on why this works so well comes from fully understanding what Cialdini calls the Law of Reciprocity.

> # Influence Tool 90
> ## *Use the Law of Reciprocity*

The Law of Reciprocity states that people generally want to return the favour when somebody does something for them first.

So powerful is the Law of Reciprocity that William Paterson actually founded a private bank based on his VP to King William III that went on to become the most powerful bank in the world.

Paterson knew what value to King William III was. Paterson did not have the value himself; he borrowed the value because he was a key person of influence.

Paterson founded the Bank of England to supply money to the King.

England had no choice but to build a powerful navy if it was to regain global power after a costly war.

Armed with a clear understanding of what value was to the King, Paterson quickly published a VP document titled *A Brief Account of the Intended Bank of England,* in which he revealed his idea of a central national bank that would help in government finances.

As there were no public funds available, in 1694 Paterson's Bank of England was set up to supply money to the King. £1.2m was raised in 12 days through Paterson's connections.

Unbelievably, not only was interest charged on the loan as you would expect, but the King actually incorporated the Bank of England, a private bank, with banking privileges including the issue of notes.

The Royal Charter was granted on 27 July 1694.

Just in case you missed it, the King needed money. Paterson created a company and plan, Paterson arranged the finances in return for interest and, in reciprocation, the King gave Paterson the monopoly on the creation of England's money supply.

Arguably, a chain of events that has had more of an influence on the world than any single event in financial history, the central banking system has been exported worldwide and became the standard monetary system.

This single piece of legislation lays the foundation for the unsustainable nature of our monetary system today and why monetary reformers like me seek to reform the consequences of this single piece of legislation and its disastrous knock-on effects on the world.

I know this is an extreme example of reciprocity in action, but an extreme example is a great way of highlighting one of the most powerful laws of influence.

One of my Banking and Finance Professional Program graduates embraced the concept of the Law of Reciprocity and VPs and started to make contact with KPIs in trading.

A few emails later he found himself in the office of a hedge fund, discussing plans with Lex van Dam, the ex-Goldman Sachs proprietary trader who created the BBC Million Dollar Traders reality TV show, where he funded newbie traders with US$1 million of his own money to run a hedge fund.

After my student had questioned Lex van Dam to find out how he could deliver value, Lex asked if he might be able to assist in a new business venture he was starting.

My student knew that I could help Lex in his new venture and the student found himself in a KPI position.

I had given value to my student in helping him with his KPI status, he gave value to Lex van Dam as he put the two of us together and we went on to discuss working together. He managed to get offers and opportunities from both Lex and myself to work together on the project.

Now all he needed to do was continue following up with further VPs and he would have found himself in the ideal scenario of being a person who makes stuff happen and perfectly lined up as soon as an opportunity presented itself.

Unfortunately, the follow-up was not combined with further VPs, but was replaced instead with lots of value extraction so the opportunity lost itself, but all my student needs to do now is continue giving value and he can win back his brownie points.

This is how it works. Keep giving value and people cannot help but reciprocate. A common mistake I see people make is expecting too much too early, which is a real shame because they have already made progress with the hardest part – making contact.

Nobody wants to be that person who never gives back, they are frowned upon in society. It will almost always come back to you and if not, just keep giving until it does, or move on (they will feel bad, so reciprocity is on your side).

Such is the power of the Law of Reciprocity that it can drive people to do some crazy things like hand over a country's monopoly on the creation of money to a private bank!

Act 2 - Demonstrate your compliance

It has become standard practice at banks and financial institutions for members of staff to qualify with the relevant professional qualification for the role in question.

Depending on which sector of banking and finance you wish to work in, the qualification is different.

For example, those pursuing a career in fund management, in most cases, would be required by the company to complete a Chartered Financial Analyst (CFA) qualification or those seeking careers in trading would need to have completed a Series 7 exam in the case of the USA, or a CISI Certificate in Investments in the case of the UK.

Different qualifications are standard in different countries.

I frequently get asked by students if they should undertake these qualifications before starting, to which I usually answer 'yes' for a number of reasons.

Firstly, it sends out a clear signal that you know what specific career you want when you have the correct qualification in the sector for which you are applying.

Secondly, you want to walk the walk and talk the talk in your niche sector in banking and finance.

A professional qualification is as good a place as any to learn the jargon.

Thirdly, when delivering VPs and closing your contacts on work opportunities you will come across the scenario where your newly-made KPI friend wants to help you out with work experience or an opportunity, but the compliance team come back and object, as it might risk the institution's status with their country's regulators if you are unregulated and unqualified.

Influence Tool 91
Use the Law of Authority

Fourthly, it is a great way of tapping into what Cialdini calls The Law of Authority, the law that states that we like to work with experts.

While a professional qualification does not make you an expert without experience, combined with some other factors it goes a long way to making you an authority in your niche.

Finally, it saves them a job, it saves them money and it makes it easier for them to hire you.

No, you don't have to do it, but those who do just what they have to do will not climb to the top, and will not be in that top 1% anyway.

So all in all, I recommend that you undertake the relevant professional qualifications as a valuable addition to your strategy.

On a side note, you can actually get a completely free guide to which professional qualifications you should be undertaking for each role in banking and finance and a guide to combining qualifications with an offer-attracting strategy by watching the free videos at **www.benedix.co.uk/qualifications**

When George Soros speaks, people listen. George Soros fully understands the Law of Authority. He prides himself on being 'somebody who insists on speaking the truth even if it's painful'.

Is it because he is a great communicator? You just need to watch one of his interviews to know that this is not the case.

He speaks with authority, and his career has reflected this. But George Soros was not always born an authority and his story is an interesting one.

Soros was a Jewish refugee from communist Hungary. Only after surviving German occupation in World War II did he build a personal fortune of many billions and become a recognised worldwide authority.

While a student at the London School of Economics, Soros worked as a railway porter and waiter.

He eventually secured an entry-level position with London merchant bank Singer and Friedlander, where he developed his theory of reflexivity during his early days in banking and finance.

He soon realised he would not make any money from his concept of reflexivity unless he went into investing on his own.

Famous for his convictions in his beliefs, he persuaded the company for which he worked at the time, Arnhold and S Bleichroeder, to set up an offshore investment fund, First Eagle, especially for him to run.

He had no track record, he was just certain that his theory would make the company money and they believed him.

His authority superseded any investment record. After proving himself in 1969, the company founded a second fund for Soros, the Double Eagle Hedge Fund.

After a successful track record, Soros then set up with his partner Jim Rogers and the rest is history.

At the time of writing, Forbes lists Soros as the 35th richest person in the world, and the 14th richest US citizen, with a net worth estimated at US$14.2 billion.

He became famous for sticking to his guns, as he demonstrated when trading against the Bank of England, making over $1 billion dollars in a day.

Soros has now become an expert, authority and respected consultant.

He said jokingly, "Well, you know, I was a human being before I became a businessman."

While George Soros earned his authority, many criticise and joke about the financial industry as people turn blindly to stockbrokers, financial advisors and experts for financial advice.

Warren Buffett once said, "Wall Street is the only place that people ride to in a Rolls Royce to get advice from those who take the subway."

So what makes us seek financial advice from those who have never invested any of their own money in the market, have not achieved any kind of financial security through investing, but have the title 'financial advisor' or 'security analyst' or 'investment specialist'?

Simple - The Law of Authority. The same reason why they are given these titles in the first place: because people like to get advice from experts – so much so that they will often ignore the credentials of what makes them the expert in the first place.

It is a law of influence that can be used for good or bad, but lack of authority is a driving force in many students and graduates failing to secure their first offer.

The right qualification, combined with results, an ED, VPs and proof can be used to overcome the authority objection.

Act 3 - Show them your Evidence Document

As mentioned in the previous chapter, your ED must be filled with proof that you have what it takes to perform in your role.

Nothing but results should be on your ED which is why I call it an Evidence Document.

Influence Tool 92
Use the Law of Social Proof

It is designed to tap into what Cialidini calls the Law of Social Proof.

The law states that we look to others in order to make judgments, especially in times of uncertainty.

This is why they look for internships and work experience with other banks, because if it is good enough for the other bank, it serves as social proof. Even if you were useless at your internship, it is social proof nonetheless.

This is why a focused, tailored relevant ED is so important. It is only meant to provide social proof for the results you can achieve, relevant to the skills that they feel are important for the role.

For example, when explaining the benefits of my Banking and Finance Professional Program, it is important to explain to interested students and graduates that thousands have been through the program, and show them the success stories of my clients who now work in most major financial institutions worldwide, because we look to others in order to make decisions in times of uncertainty.

The greatest capitalist and financier who truly tapped into the Law of Social Proof was August Belmont.

Belmont used the power of social proof to put an end to the Panic of 1837 and save America's banks on the verge of bankruptcy.

This incredible story began when Belmont found himself sweeping floors, polishing furniture and running errands for the Rothschilds.

The House of Rothschild had established European banking and finance houses from the late 18th century.

It has been argued that the Rothschild family as a whole possesses by far the largest private fortune in the world in modern history.

Realising that sweeping floors for the Rothschilds was an ideal opportunity, by age 17 he was actually handling successful negotiations for the family.

Aged 21, he boarded the first trip to New York in the midst of the Panic of 1837.

With fierce ambition, he used the social proof and name of the Rothschild family.

So strong was the Rothschild name that his association meant that anyone and everyone extended him credit.

He immediately used the credit and social proof to set up August Belmont and Company and began buying in the depressed market when nobody else could.

Through the social proof of the Rothschild association, he was granted unlimited loans even when lenders wouldn't grant each other credit.

In this remarkable turn of events he got America lending again. With the credit he bought stocks, commodities and bank notes, halting the panic and making him a hero of his time.

Social proof is a powerful concept and, as you build your KPI status, your ED should be filled with social proof, while others see it as a record of achievement to showcase their academic achievements and list their roles and duties like all the others following the traditional books.

One of my Banking and Finance Professional Program graduates, Alex, actually got ten calls in one day from banks and financial institutions on the first day that we added a touch of social proof to his ED. Prior to turning the CV into an ED it had been posted on job boards for six months with no response at all.

By having a business angel who is one of the most respected businessmen in banking and finance, Peter Hargreaves, the Law of Social Proof has been an invaluable tool in growing my businesses, purely because of the Law of Social Proof.

Be armed and ready with your ED as opportunity knocks.

Act 4 - Get feedback on your work together

After delivering value and warming up to a pitch, a close or a request, it is very important that you seek out what the person you are attempting to pitch to is interested in.

Influence Tool 93
Ask people more questions rather than talking about yourself

I have found questions to be one of the most powerful tools of influence.

Questions allow you to find out what is on other people's minds, what they are interested in, what they are looking for, how your VP went, what their hobbies are and other extremely valuable information.

The easiest way of connecting with somebody is simply asking them questions about what they are interested in and finding that point of common interest.

So before you deliver your pitch, use questions to find out where they are and steer them in the direction you want them to go.

Influence Tool 94
Use the Law of Liking

Questions also allow you to tap into one of the six laws of influence in Cialdini's book – The Law of Liking.

People like to do business with and employ people who are similar to themselves, or similar to how they would like to be.

People do not like to do business with or employ people who are not like themselves or who are not how they would like to be.

Nobody understood the Law of Liking better than Bertis Charles Forbes, the Scottish financial journalist and author who founded Forbes magazine.

Understanding the power of being one of those people that others just like, you could say that he connected his way to the top through schmoozing and charm.

He was one of those people that you just could not say 'no' to.

Forbes specialised in writing biographical accounts on the most influential business leaders, focusing on the positive traits that led them to success.

Influence Tool 95
Only talk about the positive aspects of other people

He fully understood the old saying 'If you don't have anything nice to say, then don't say anything at all' and was an example to all about how far this could get you.

For example, Forbes spoke of Charles M Schwab as a man who has 'played the business game' and won 'an unusual measure of happiness and an extraordinary number of friends'.

The secret to Forbes' success can be found in the traits Forbes valued most in life when writing about others.

He wrote: 'Schwab, from the start, had goodwill in his heart towards his workers and his associates ... he has never lost sight of the fundamental fact that, in the end, a wealth of friends means more than a wealth of gold'.

You could say Forbes capitalised on schmoozing with Wall Street's most notorious business leaders – such as bankers A P Giannini, the founder of Bank of America and George F Baker, the co-founder of the First National Bank of the City of New York.

Forbes did not inherit the connections, he earned them.

Back then, tycoons generally kept to themselves, rarely responding to stockbrokers and even more rarely to reporters.

When starting out, Forbes rented a room at a Wall Street hotel and would network with Wall Streeters at the hotel bar. He blended in with tycoons and later became one of them by fully harnessing the Law of Liking.

From a poor background, Forbes scraped together every cent possible and journeyed to Manhattan in 1904 where he worked for free for the Journal of Commerce to get his foot in the door.

After being hired as financial editor, he started Forbes in 1917. His name became so strong that it made the magazine.

He inspired the world with his words and was a true advocate of self-responsibility and reputation.

Forbes said, "The man who is intent on making the most of his opportunities is too busy to bother about luck."

Implement the Law of Liking and you will not find yourself short of opportunity; leave the negative blogging and moaning to the 99%, the 1% who will climb to the top cannot afford to be associated with cheap shots at the expense of others.

Another of my Platinum Plus Partners wanted to become the KPI in fund management and we developed a plan to connect her with some of the greatest fund managers in the world by writing a book called The Greatest Minds In Fund Management.

This is truly tapping into the Law of Liking and using a clever strategy to become a KPI.

If you contacted 100 fund managers through a clever referral strategy and asked them to be interviewed as part of the book The Greatest Minds In Fund Management, would some of them want to connect with you?

This worked because we developed a referral process where she could utilise some of my fund management KPI contacts from my network; she had the authority and social proof to be taken seriously.

We also made sure she knew the right people to get the book published and launched to make it a guaranteed success.

As she completes the book for launch she is truly becoming a KPI in the fund management industry, with a killer ED and a big choice of contacts to close. She is selecting the opportunity while everybody else is struggling with graduate scheme applications.

Once we launch the book together successfully, she will also have proof of results to add to her ED.

As she is a Platinum Plus Partner of mine, I will make the book a success for her, that is how it works.

So just before you pitch, remember to use questions to connect, build rapport and find out how well your VP went.

The Law of Liking is a powerful concept that can be used for tremendous benefit in your journey to the top.

Act 5 - Deliver your pitch

If you have followed my steps up until now, moving from questioning to pitching will be a seamless transition.

If you have genuinely delivered value, it is now time to explain confidently and congruently that there is more where that came from and that you are looking to add more value on an on-going basis.

You have overcome the 'compliance objection' by qualifying in the right field, you have overcome the 'no experience objection' by delivering results in advance through your VP, you have overcome the 'proof of results objection' with your ED and you have delivered social proof through your networks and KPI status.

Now get honest with them and tell them what you want and why you have been doing all this work.

As an investment banker, I get to see countless pitches and see first-hand the difference between an awful pitch and a great pitch.

The main difference is the awful pitches focus on what the pitcher wants; great ones focus on what the person you are pitching to wants.

Quite simply, the more you know about the person to whom you are pitching – their wants, needs, wounds and pain – the better you can solve the problems with your solution and labour.

Another important point on pitching is not to make the mistake of only pitching to KPIs. You never know who are talking to and as a KPI you want to treat everyone with respect. Most people that you will be pitching to have a trusted side-kick who filters VPs for them.

Very often the receptionist can be the key to your success. I have a trusted side-kick who followed this exact strategy and created more value than anyone I have ever worked with. His VPs, results in advance and unconditional loyalty have made him an indispensable asset.

Any students or graduates who send me VPs must first get past my trusted side-kick, Jal Islam. He is a shining example of how never to allow lack of opportunity to be an issue ever again. He earned himself a role as one of the head consultants who gave so much value that I eventually reciprocated by giving him equity in Metal Monkey Private Equity. Now he gets to work with some of the biggest high flyers and has a phone book that most would kill to get their hands on.

Huge rewards can come a lot faster than most when you adopt these principles.

> ## Influence Tool 96
> *Use the Law of Commitment and Consistency*

The beauty is that through this process you have already tapped into another of Cialdini's six laws of influence – The Law of Commitment and Consistency.

The law states that people will do more to remain consistent with their commitments and beliefs if they have already taken a small step.

Because they have allowed you to deliver value for them, they have already made a small commitment to working with you.

If they pull out now and don't work with you further, it will be going against the Law of Commitment and Consistency.

They want to remain consistent with their commitment that working with you might be a good idea.

They have taken responsibility just by accepting your VP.

Now they want you to prove them right for working with you in the first place and all laws are stacked in your favour.

When you stack six laws of influence in your favour like this, something is going to happen at some point.

So now is your time to pitch for experience.

Mike Harris, when pitching to Prudential for £80 million in order to fund what was the world's largest internet-only bank,

Egg, developed a framework and architecture to deliver consistent results called the 'perfect pitch'.

Mike Harris actually gave an exclusive one-off training session for my students and graduates on creating the perfect pitch at one of my Banking and Finance Millionaires events.

The recording is available as part of my Climbing To The Top Program for Banking and Finance Professional Program graduates where he reveals his formulas for the perfect pitch for students and graduates pitching to CEOs and contacts.

The key to the pitch is to make it short and cover only the information that the person is most interested in.

Influence Tool 97
Know everything about the person to whom you are pitching or being interviewed by

---

When preparing for my pitch with Peter Hargreaves, I immediately set out to find out everything I could about Peter Hargreaves himself.

I read his books, I opened a self-invested personal pension with his wealth management company Hargreaves Lansdown and I tailored everything I said to what I knew were his core values and interests.

I looked for signals for when I was going off track and, most importantly, I asked questions to gauge his response and only continued discussing the things that he wanted to know rather than what I wanted to tell him.

I am assuming that you are only pitching to people that you are genuinely interested in working with; if you use these techniques and they are fake, people will spot you a mile off.

Again, constructing the perfect pitch is a whole book in itself and we can only touch upon the surface here.

I recommend learning this skill now, as it will serve you on your whole journey to the top and none better to learn from than Mike Harris himself.

Act 6 - Add a touch of scarcity

Now that you have delivered value and delivered your pitch, the closing touch is to give them, very subtly, a little bit of fear of loss.

Here is one more for Luck...
Influence Tool 98
Use the Law of Scarcity

It is important for your contact to know you have other things going on too.

Be very careful though, only use this if it is true and use with caution. You don't want to make them think you are arrogant or don't appreciate working with them.

The value you have delivered has to go somewhere, though, and you would like it to go to them by working with them, but you are a KPI and you are connected so if it does not go to them, your value will go somewhere else.

Now be very careful not to go too aggressive on the scarcity; you want them to know you want to work with them, but a simple comment at the end of your pitch will pull the odds in your favour if you have genuinely created demand for yourself.

Let them know that you are putting yourself on the market and because you have done business with them before, you did it because it would be your dream come true to work with them, but if it is not possible you have had interest from their competition.

Of course it goes without saying that this has to be true, and if you have pitched to somebody else, then it is true.

The Law of Scarcity Cialdini demonstrates drives people crazy to make decisions out of their fear of missing out.

It happens to us all. We are much more likely to buy the last cake in the store out of fear that somebody else might get it.

I am guessing here, but when somebody has a track record of creating the first telephone bank and has two billion-dollar start-ups under his wing, when he pitches to you for the first ever internet bank, a little part of you fears that he will get funding from someone else and you will miss out.

I don't know, but I am sure the Prudential board felt a little bit of the Law of Scarcity when Mike Harris pitched his third billion-pound turnover business idea that turned out to be a great investment after all.

So there you have it, the 'Six Act Play' in motion. There is more to it, but my goal was to highlight some of the laws of influence through an example strategy.

So let's recap why this works so well to close contacts into work experience opportunities.

1. **You are tapping into the Law of Reciprocity by delivering value and asking nothing in return, giving a clear demonstration of results in advance when you successfully deliver on your proposition.**

2. **You have shown your authority in your niche sector by qualifying yourself in the specific role and mastering the jargon, overcoming the 'compliance objection'.**

3. **You have plenty of social proof by constructing your ED in the correct way.**

4. **You have tapped into the Law of Liking by questioning and getting feedback from the contact (now friend) for whom you have delivered value.**

5. You have successfully pitched in a way that makes your contact stay committed and consistent by working with you in the first place, tapping into the Law of Commitment and Consistency.

6. You have tapped into the Law of Scarcity by demonstrating that you are a sought-after candidate, and if you have delivered value correctly they will believe you.

Use with caution. It is a very powerful concept that has delivered consistent results for many seeking their first break in banking and finance.

As I mentioned in the beginning of this chapter, this is an introduction to the topic of influence and I strongly recommend investing in mastering these skills to serve you forever in your journey to the top.

So we are approaching the end of the book and it has been amazing sharing these ideas with you.

You now understand that you need a clear map for climbing to the top. You know how important it is to know what you want. You know you need to be willing to do it and what will be involved. You know you need to follow your passion. You are going to build the evidence to develop a belief that you can do it. You know that you are going to have to dare to be different and you now know that the only skill to make it to the top is your ability to influence.

So what now?

CHAPTER EIGHT

Do It In Service

influence
your way to the
top in banking
and finance

> *And the final 'Cherry on the cake' bonus...*
> ## Influence Tool 99
> ### *Attach your mission to great causes*

As your journey to the top progresses, one day you will probably write your words in a book much like I am now.

As your mission unfolds it becomes apparent that your duty is to live in service.

By service I mean as you become a shining example for others to look up to, as more and more seek your words for inspiration, as your story unfolds, you realise that others need your help.

As my mission unfolds it becomes apparent that, at the end of the day, we can add value to the world or we can extract value, and there is no in-between.

If you are not adding, you are extracting.

It becomes a duty to fulfill my mission because I have attached the meaning of its achievement to so many big causes that will have a genuine impact on the world.

Once you attach your mission to important causes outside of yourself, it no longer becomes about you, it becomes about the difference you are going to make in the world.

I believe that we all want to make a difference, to pass away knowing that we stamped our mark on the world and to feel special, an inspiration to others.

When you attach your mission to causes that will make a difference in the world, no matter how small, your mission becomes something where you have to find the strength to deal with the criticism, where you have to find a way to overcome the huge problems ahead, where you have to discipline yourself to handle the rejection and where you have to build the emotional muscle to develop that sense of certainty that, no matter what, you will find the strength to achieve what you know is possible.

It makes it easier to muster up the energy to break through the barriers and climb to the top when you do it in service.

If there is a secret, I think this is it: do it in service to the world and benefit personally as you help others.

My mission cannot fail because great causes rely on me for funding.

My mission cannot fail because I get Facebook emails every day from students who were feeling depressed and have now found new hope in their careers.

My mission cannot fail because I am a patron for a cause called 'Peace One Day', founded by one of the most inspirational people I know, Jeremy Gilley.

If you ever need inspiration and a shining example of what it takes to climb to the top, then watch one of his videos at **www.peaceoneday.org**

It will soon make you realise what one person can achieve from nothing, when you find the strength and attach yourself to a mission that is greater than yourself.

My mission cannot fail because I am a patron for Jeremy Gilley's organisation that created the first day of global ceasefire and non-violence on September 21st that has saved millions of lives (mark it in your diary, this is a global day to celebrate peace).

How can I let something as small as rejection stop me?

My mission cannot fail because I have convinced some of the richest businessmen in the UK that I will do it and I don't want to be the guy that lets a Peter Hargreaves or a Mike Harris down.

My mission cannot fail because monetary reform will have a huge impact on third world debt, the happiness of our nation and on international relations, as well as putting an end to the inevitable boom and bust trap we are in right now as we inflate and deflate our economy, sending people from debt into bankruptcy in order to manage our money supply.

I cannot let my own insecurities get in the way.

My mission cannot fail because our monetary system is so destructive and unnecessary I cannot let people's criticism get in the way.

My mission cannot fail because eventually I want my bank to help those who need it the most through microfinancing.

I just need to think of those who have worked their way out of poverty every time I get overwhelmed with the amount of work I am taking on.

My mission cannot fail because all these factors combined dwarf the simple self-interest of financial abundance and the need for significance.

Of course, those are driving forces; we all deserve financial abundance and to feel special, but the need to contribute outside of oneself is greater than any force and leads to more fulfilment than anything else.

Once you have committed yourself this far, your mission cannot fail. At the very least, you will be remembered as that person that never gave up.

Harness your inherent human need to contribute to the world and you have a force so powerful, so dynamic, so strong that you will find all the resources around you to handle the road ahead.

As you secure your ideal career, as your unique contribution unfolds, as your purpose manifests, as you climb to the top, as you make a difference, never forget why you are doing it.

All of a sudden getting that job seems like an easy task, doesn't it?

Enjoy the journey and please join my Facebook group How To Get A Job In The City and post a comment on the wall about one commitment that you have decided to take right now to make sure you begin your journey from student to CEO and beyond.

Always commit yourself while you are in a state of high emotion and strength to keep you committed when the momentum and emotion is slipping slightly.

I can't wait to hear your story and I hope to join you one day in the future, either through one of my training programs or through a mutually beneficial VP and partnership.

Earn more, achieve more, climb to the top...

...but do it in service, and you cannot fail!

Final Exercise

Answer these questions without doing any further research, just jot down your first answer.

Take a journal and go through this book and hand-write each of the 97 tools of influence in order to hard-wire them into your brain.

Carry them with you and reflect each day upon what they mean to you, one at a time.

Teach them to others and refer back to this book to jog your memory of what they mean.

Once written out in full, claim your free training videos at www.BankingAndFinanceProgram.com

Leave a comment under the videos and let me know what you think. I read them all personally.

Influence Tool 100
This one is yours to fill in...

_____

_____

_____

_____

_____

1387608R0

Printed in Great Britain by
Amazon.co.uk, Ltd.,
Marston Gate.